FORAGER

Forager

Field Notes for Surviving a Family Cult

Michelle Dowd

Illustrations by Susan Brand

ALGONQUIN BOOKS
OF CHAPEL HILL
2023

Published by

ALGONQUIN BOOKS OF CHAPEL HILL
Post Office Box 2225
Chapel Hill, North Carolina 27515-2225

an imprint of WORKMAN PUBLISHING CO., INC.,
a subsidiary of HACHETTE BOOK GROUP, INC.
1290 Avenue of the Americas,
New York, NY 10104

The nutritional information, recipes, and instructions contained within this book have been
created based on the author's own experiences and are in no way intended as a substitute
for medical counseling. All recommendations are made without guarantee on the part of the
author or Algonquin Books. The author and publisher disclaim any liability in connection
with the use of this information. In particular, eating wild plants (and fungi) is inherently risky.
Plants can be easily mistaken and individuals vary in their physiological reactions to plants
that are touched or consumed.

The publisher is not responsible for websites
(or their content) that are not owned by the publisher.

Library of Congress Cataloging-in-Publication Data

Names: Dowd, Michelle, [date]– author. | Brand, Susan (Illustrator), illustrator.
Title: Forager : field notes on surviving a family cult / Michelle Dowd ;
illustrations by Susan Brand.
Description: First edition. | Chapel Hill : Algonquin Books of Chapel Hill, 2023. |
Summary: "A memoir of the author's experience growing up in
an apocalyptic cult, with an emphasis on how understanding the natural
world was her key to escape and survival"— Provided by publisher.
Identifiers: LCCN 2022040157 | ISBN 9781643751856 (hardcover) |
ISBN 9781643753713 (ebook)
Subjects: LCSH: Dowd, Michelle, [date]– | Christian sects—California. | Adult child abuse
victims—United States—Biography. | Ex-cultists—United States—Biography. |
Wilderness survival—California. | Angeles National Forest (Calif.)
Classification: LCC BX9998.D68 A3 2023 | DDC 299/.93092 [B]—dc23/eng/20221118
LC record available at https://lccn.loc.gov/2

10 9 8 7 6 5 4 3 2 1
First Edition

For my mother
(1942–2022)

AUTHOR'S NOTE

THIS IS A WORK OF MEMORY, but I have done my best to tell a truthful story. I met with all my siblings, several of my cousins, my parents, two of my aunts, dozens of former members of the Field, and several current ones (including the current director) to render as accurately as possible what the Field was like from 1976 to 1986 in the context of collective memory. While the Field, begun by my grandfather in 1931, still exists, it has been renamed and I've been told it is a radically different organization from the one I grew up in.

I have used details (and dialogue) from several of the catalogs, notebooks, and diaries I kept throughout my childhood and adolescence, numerous letters I saved from Luke, and my mother's books and notes. I have been corrected on some points, mostly of chronology, and have adjusted to get as close as I can to what really happened.

The nutritional information, recipes, and instructions contained within this book were created based on my experiences and my mother's teachings and are in no way intended as a guide on how to eat in the wild. Eating wild plants and fungi is inherently risky. Plants can be easily mistaken and individuals vary in their physiological reactions to touching and consuming plants. And so the information included here should not be used without professional training.

I have changed the names of everyone except my grandmother Ruth, her siblings Bernice and Oscar, her nephew Gary, Dr. Shore, my hospital roommates Sandra and Gayle, the docent Barbara, and all of the dogs.

For 99.9 percent of the time since our species came to be, we were hunters and foragers . . . We were bounded only by the Earth and the ocean and the sky.

—CARL SAGAN

Introduction

I GREW UP ON A MOUNTAIN, preparing for the Apocalypse.

This doesn't explain the juxtaposition of faith and famine, or how the landscape of my childhood was more amorphous than the boundary of a mountain implies, but it's the simplest truth for which I can find words.

For a decade of my childhood, the Mountain was the closest thing I had to a home, and I learned to forage for what I needed to survive on it.

But my real home wasn't a place. It was an idea. An idea my maternal grandfather turned into an organization we called the Field, a closed community both my mother and I were born into, which expanded over the decades onto the mountain upon which I grew up. Both Field and Mountain were governed by Grandpa, the ruler of our world.

Grandpa said he was God's prophet and would live to be five hundred years old, that the angels would descend from heaven and take him up into the clouds like Elijah. Grandpa's followers believed every word he said, because at the Field, he was the only one with authority. His pontifications were the soundtrack of my childhood, and his sincere belief that God's vengeance would be unleashed upon the world unless a small group of God's chosen people stayed his hand terrified me. Because we were those people. And as his granddaughter, I had inherited the divine right and responsibility to lead.

From the age of seven to seventeen, I lived on the Mountain, a sixteen-acre undeveloped camp sitting on the San Andreas Fault, in the central section of the Transverse Ranges, within the Angeles National Forest. My maternal grandfather had obtained a lease for this site under a special use permit from the US Forest Service in 1947, ostensibly to run a camp for boys. He had dreamed of developing the land into a little enclave of worship amid the surrounding seven hundred thousand acres of national forest, but when he found a piece of property available in nearby Arcadia, he put his energy into developing the Field there instead.

They say the basin of land in Southern California where the Field is located was a community dump when Grandpa acquired it in 1951, having convinced a sympathetic businessman to lease it to him for one dollar a year. My father and several other boys who were teenagers at the time cleaned it up and built clubrooms and a church hall out of cinder block. They built a brick cross and painted it white, and constructed a stained-glass mural featuring the words *Feed My Lambs*.

The physical space of the Field opens at the end of a suburban cul-de-sac. There is only one way in and one way out. The small entryway leads down a hill to the basin, now covered in ballfields and a smattering of clubrooms. A pavilion gym, which also serves as a church, was erected in 1979. Leaders live in little homes along the bank of the property.

In the 1970s, the Mountain was approximately a two-hour drive from the Field, and moving there alone with our nuclear family gave my mother distance and license to explore a space away from her father's watchful eye. During our ten years there, she taught my siblings and me to love and care for the land while taking up arms against Satan, the earth's ruler. But she also believed that, like Abraham, she was called to sacrifice her children as a testament to her devotion to her Lord; in exchange, God would bless her, and he would multiply her seed *as the stars of the heaven, and as the sand which is upon the sea shore;* and her seed would *possess the gate of his enemies.*

So we memorized scripture, put on the armor of God, and bowed to the mercurial tyranny of Grandpa, to whom we belonged. Mother sacrificed us, and like Abraham's son Isaac, we survived her sacrifice, and multiplied her seed.

When we moved to the Mountain, my three siblings and I lived with our parents in a one-room mess hall that was already on the land Grandpa had leased. We slept on army bunks, walked down the hill to the outhouse, and foraged for seeds. We were told the end of the world was imminent and we needed to be prepared. Part of that preparation was learning to survive off what the Mountain would yield. The other part was becoming a soldier in the army of God.

MOTHER TAUGHT US TO CULL from the forest floor, how to identify and consume yerba santa, yucca, prickly pear, nettles, elderberry, snow plant, dandelion, rose hips, chokecherry, gooseberry, and the seeds, pollen, bark, and sap of Jeffrey, pinyon, sugar, Coulter, and knobcone pine trees and black oak trees. I know what you can eat raw and what you have to pound, grind down, dry, or bake. I know the ratios to dilute, how far to dig during a drought, and what is worth fighting for.

Mother explained how warming temperatures were allowing bark beetles to infiltrate Jeffrey pines, whose seeds we consumed. She saw the destruction of ecosystems as the biblical Apocalypse, and she prepared us to survive the harsh conditions Armageddon would bring. She taught us to sleep on the bare earth, and when water wasn't available, to siphon dew from leaves or distill urine in a pit. She taught us to trust the layers of sustenance hidden in places humans hadn't yet appropriated as their own.

I didn't choose to be born at the Field, nor do I accept Grandpa's fundamentalist ideologies, leadership, rules, or vision as true, and I don't want his story next to mine, even now. The Mountain holds his stories too—in the rocks, in the foundation of the buildings, in the plaques on the walls—but I will not be telling Grandpa's story. His followers have their version, and they continue to tell it, heralding him as a hero.

That is not my story.

Mother told us her father spoke the voice of God, and she still insists that his words were true, and that his vision was our birthright, our legacy, and our responsibility to carry forth, like a torch in the darkness of this world.

When she heard I was writing a book, she forbade me from criticizing her father or the Field. "I will not allow you to destroy the organization our family has spent lifetimes building. How could you do this to me? I forbid you from writing this. I won't allow it."

I assured her that my book isn't really about Grandpa, and that I won't reveal her secrets. The story I'm writing is mine.

"This is your family," she admonished. "You have to keep our secrets safe. It's your duty."

Where does her story end and mine begin?

THE MOUNTAIN IS THE ONLY PLACE my mother calls home, although she hasn't been back to it in years. She can't breathe on her own anymore, but she says that as long as she is attached to a tank of oxygen and doesn't cavort above sea level, she feels fine. She is in the advanced stages of pulmonary fibrosis, which means the scarring in her lungs is expanding and blocking her capacity for breath, the final constriction of which is now inevitable. Higher altitudes haven't been accessible to her for several years.

She says she has no regrets, that she has lived the life God asked her to.

I've been saying goodbye to Mother for many months, sitting with her during a hospice that keeps getting renewed and extended. While she lies dying, I look through her King James Bible, hoping to find her secrets. I am careful with the scraps of paper she has inserted throughout, and make two stacks: a pile from the Old Testament and a pile from the New.

As she sleeps, I unfold each of the papers, one by one, looking for a point of entry into who she might be on the inside, separate from the mask she wears when she communicates with me. I can't tell if she's in pain. Mother can scream with her mouth closed. As can I.

I'm careful as I unfold the scraps, as if I am opening treasure maps. What I discover doesn't make sense to me. They are all drawings of the backs of people's heads. I used to watch her sketch these various heads of hair while we were in church or in the hospital or watching Dad's games. She said it was the only thing she could draw with the tools she had. One of the sketches has long, curly blond hair. It looks like it could be me.

Mother believes we are tool-using animals who have been on this earth for about six thousand years. I've told her our human ancestors began as pack animals over 2.5 million years ago, and for most of the time since, we were integrated into the natural world as hunter-gatherers. When I say things like this, she changes the subject or hangs up the phone, so I'm hesitant to bring it up again.

I want to tell her how the hundreds of thousands of ancestral generations we spent as wildlife are more imprinted into us, even now, than the relatively few we've spent developing agriculture and permanent settlements. If she knew this, it might make sense to her why the natural world is the place she knows so deeply in her DNA; why, even though she was born and raised in Pasadena, the Mountain is the only place that feels like home.

During these visits, she tells me I'm nothing like her, says that when I turned my back on my calling, I left behind everything she tried to teach me. But she is wrong. I've assembled an entire life from foraging.

I left the Mountain and the Field, but I am still my mother's daughter. When I am hungry, I know where to look to find what I need: shelter, fire, signaling, water, food. Signal when you have hope of rescue. Avoid drawing attention when you don't. Don't feel sorry for yourself. Don't cry. Pain is inevitable. Learn to move through it.

Build a shelter. Gather what you need to build a fire. Construct a signaling apparatus. Find a source of water. If you are not rescued, you will have time to find food later. For now, you must focus on what will sustain, not satiate you.

Focus on what's in front of you, not on what you want. Focus on what you can see. Survey the landscape. Triangulate to pinpoint a location to build your nest. Identify the materials that will provide the best shelter. Do this before nightfall. Do this now.

Use everything. Waste nothing. Remember that rules are guidelines, not absolutes. Get to know the intricacies of the land, like the intricacies of your body. You can take what you need and leave the rest behind.

WHEN I WAS NINE, my friend and I rescued a baby duckling and nurtured him back to health along the Mississippi River. Grandpa often pulled me or one of my siblings away from the Mountain, one at a time, to go on "the Trip," one of the annual months-long cross-country proselytizing excursions members of the Field took via caravan each summer. Some of the trips were for girls at the Field, so we could become godly wives and mothers. On the girls' version of the Trip, Grandpa put Mother at the helm. One thing I liked about Mother being in charge is that animals were always included, especially ones that needed rescue.

When we found the abandoned duck, we were traveling the southern states in a group caravan of nine large vehicles, driven by Grandpa's most trusted disciples. Every night we pulled into a new campground, we set up our tents, constructed an elaborate set from a semitrailer, and put on a mildly veiled Christian musical called *The Last Torch*.

We loved Sippi the duck and we coddled him, and because he had imprinted on us, we believed he loved us in return.

We didn't want to put Sippi in a cage, so we made a small leash with a soft, wide leather loop that hung gently around his neck. We took turns leading him, though it was hardly necessary, because everywhere we went, Sippi followed willingly.

We were two little girls with one little duck between us, and for a few weeks, we saw ourselves as maternal. We walked with tender pride along the river, radiant with the kind of confidence that comes from being needed.

I wish I could tell you that as Sippi grew, we began to feel more and more ridiculous, leading him around campgrounds on a leash, that eventually he began to pay more attention to the natural world around him than to us, and we realized we were holding him back from being a wild duck. I want to tell you we shooed him away along the river, watched him approach other ducks with trepidation, waited patiently until he was ready, cheering when he flapped his wings and flew toward the others, that we watched him go, crying hot self-sacrificial tears.

Some goodbyes are like that.

But the truth is, Sippi died in a campground while he was still a duckling. We let him eat from the grass wherever we went, and one day he got sick. It was probably from pesticides sprayed on the dandelions, or it could have been a poisonous weed we didn't recognize, but one afternoon, he didn't want to follow us. He went limp that night, and we held him and watched him convulse until he was stiff, eyeballs open, judging us.

Some goodbyes are like that.

I have been to healers who wrapped me in blankets and guided me in meditations about trees and lakes and sun and shelter. Then we drank tea in silence and practiced communicating kindness with the language of our bodies. I have followed the recommendations of friends and acquaintances like bread crumbs, letting myself be punctured by needles, accepting energy exchanges and reiki and Thai massages in safe spaces. One healer gave me holy water from her refrigerator and chanted as I sipped from it. She said I was in the midst of an archetype shift, that I needed to let go of sanctioned scripts.

Now I look straight at the sun and let it burn into the hollow spaces where I used to be.

I wanted my goodbye to the Mountain to be clean, the way I've imagined saying goodbye to Sippi could have been clean, certain that his freedom in the world was preferable to being attached to us.

Not all goodbyes are like that.

Some people think leaving a cult is like shedding preadolescence, entering into a grown-up body free from the bonds of oppression. But when I think of my preadolescence, I picture a little girl dead on the Mississippi River, eyes wide and stiff. My innocence was over long before I met Sippi, but when I look back, I wish one of us had flown free.

Freeing oneself is the first step; claiming ownership of that freed self has been a lifelong journey.

AMID THE PINE TREES in the Angeles National Forest, my ten-year-old self has just risen and is staring down the mountain. All night, in the brisk and shallow restlessness of early spring, I think of her and her inner compass, incomplete, navigating space with the tools she has been given.

This girl has been indoctrinated by a cult, but she has a high pain tolerance and a basic knowledge of the region's ecosystem. She doesn't know that this isn't yet enough to get her anywhere. But she knows it's enough to survive where she is.

I think of her sharpening her mind against the silence of the trees. Whatever will be coming up the mountain, she is watching, breathing, and tasting with her wordless love.

This ten-year-old girl is not on a wilderness adventure. She hasn't packed what she will need to be safe and comfortable. Dozens of books could have taught her how to do this effectively, but she hasn't chosen this adventure, she doesn't have access to books, and she isn't attached to the idea of safety.

Here is what she knows. If you find yourself lost in the wilderness without any protective gear, without a flashlight, a compass, a knife, matches, a water bottle, a sleeping bag, or even a jacket, the only real tool you have is your mind.

Your prospects of surviving increase if you look at nature as a place to belong.

The girl belongs nowhere, but she can find a way to belong

anywhere. Wherever she is, she knows how to stay calm, and to differentiate between wants and needs.

She knows that within minutes of the onset of survival stress, the attitude she develops will make the difference between life and death. The story she tells herself about her situation will determine how she adapts to her new environment and its changing conditions. She doesn't feel lost, even when she doesn't know where she is. Nothing in her spatial memory matches what she sees, but lost is an emotional state, and she is not emotional.

She knows that most people who are lost make things worse for themselves. They feel claustrophobic, as if their surroundings are closing in on them, so they run or wander frantically in a direction that takes them back to where they started, unaware that humans are prone to circular movement. When you are afraid, you can't solve problems or figure out what to do, so people who are lost fail to notice landmarks, or fail to remember them, and they lose track of how far they've traveled, and in which direction.

If you are lost, stay put.

She is not afraid. She knows that even when you think you have nothing, everything around you is an invisible web of information, and that is always something.

Usually, it is enough.

You can find what you need anywhere. You just have to know what you're looking for.

Yerba Santa

Yerba santa, also known as holy weed, grows 3 to 4 feet tall. Its leaves are 3 to 4 inches long, and often sticky with resin. Its flowers are white, lavender, or darker purple, and shaped like little trumpets.

The leathery, lance-shaped leaves can be chewed fresh, and they taste sweeter the longer you chew them. Dry or fresh leaves can be mashed into a poultice or used to brew tea. Yerba santa has been used to treat respiratory conditions, including coughs, colds, and swelling of the airways, as well as fever and dry mouth. Some people use it to relieve muscle spasms and to loosen phlegm.

To make tea, place 3 leaves (fresh or dry) into a cup with boiling water and let it steep for 15 minutes before drinking.

"DON'T TELL ANYONE, but your cousin is with God now."

We are driving in a snowstorm and Mother is speaking to us from the helm. It's a January evening, and we've been on the road in our Buick Estate for almost three hours, making our way from the Field to the Mountain, where we live.

We can barely see the road, and Mother is tense.

"What cousin?" I ask. All of our cousins live at the Field, and all of them were alive a few hours ago.

"You know, Gary," she says. "But it's for the best."

We've met Gary only once. He's Great-Aunt Bernice's grandson, which I think makes him like a second or third cousin or something, and he's had leukemia for years. He's much older than us, like maybe even twenty. In any case, he was a full-grown man, and already saved by Jesus, so he's living in a heavenly mansion now and there's no reason to feel sad.

All of us are hungry, and we are listening to Mother in the dark, because she says the light inside makes it hard for her to see. She hates driving, even on a good day, but since Dad is already up on the Mountain, caring for the Field boys, who are all there learning about God, away from the temptations of the world, Mother has to drive.

She doesn't say anything else on the subject, so the four of us go back to shoving one another and whispering through our teeth, until she turns around and yells, "Stop!"

The Buick spins and plunges into a snowbank.

We aren't wearing seat belts, so some of us are thrown onto the floor; others, over the front seat into the windshield, with a thud. Mother shouts out, "Roll call!" and our voices ring out in succession: "One." "Two." "Three." "Four." I am ten years old, and this is not my first crash.

The road is dark, but we are still on it, shoved sideways into the bank of snow, all the way up to the front windshield. We sit quietly, because Mother doesn't like noise.

"We'll hike up," she says. "Bring everything with you."

We try to look at one another, but it is too dark to read expressions.

"I'm hungry," our five-year-old brother whines.

"Pack your stuff," Mother orders.

Headlights blind us. A car has turned the bend and is driving toward us, close enough to plow into us, as we watch. But it stops, headlights pointed boldly through our side windows, flooding the car with light. The engine stays on, but someone is getting out of the car. We can't tell who it is. The lights are shining in on us, and the figure is out there, moving forward.

"Lock the doors," Mother says, and we each reach for the door closest to us, manually pressing down the knobs. Then we duck, every one of us, lying on the seats or the floor, breathing quietly, as if we can hide.

We have been taught to be wary of Outsiders, and we are used to hiding. But I can tell: this time it won't work.

I hear a knock. I am still up front, propelled from the impact. I look up from where I am huddled on the floor and see the figure knocking on the passenger window. Mother doesn't speak, so we don't either.

A man's face is pressed against the glass, and he can clearly make out that there are bodies inside this car. "Are you okay in there?" his voice booms. "Is everyone okay in there?"

We wait in silence. He tries to pry open the door, jiggling the car. I hope we look dead and he will go away.

He doesn't.

Mother's head is down. The man is still knocking.

"Michelle," she whispers, "go get help from your father. We'll wait here."

I lift my head to look at her, and the light floods her face. "Go," she says. "Lock the door behind you."

I glance at the man without moving, then reach up to unlock the door. I use my body weight to slam it into him hard, to push him back far enough to allow me to slide out of the car, then quickly lock the door again before I slam it shut and scramble away from the car.

The man is not as large as my father, or, really, any of the men I have grown up around, but he is quick. "Wait," he says. He grabs my jacket. I almost slip out of it, but the voice is gentle. "Child, wait. I'm here to help you."

His tone stops my momentum, and I land on my knees in the snow. We aren't more than three feet from the family car, but I know I am in this alone.

"Let me help you."

I am used to the culture of army men, direct and gruff. I'm not sure how to respond to this man's kindness. Surely,

Mother is watching, judging my choices. The road is quiet. I wonder if she can hear us, or if she is blocking this out, as she often does when she doesn't want to see what is happening around her.

I stand up and try to show some confidence. "It's okay, sir. I can go get our father. We don't need help." And I walk toward the far right side of the road, snow up past my tennis shoes and rubbing against the flesh of my ankles with each step.

"Wait!" he calls out. But I am ahead of him now, hurrying up the dark road.

I know this mountain. And even on this cloud-covered night, in the white blur of snowfall, I know my way. I don't look back.

But I haven't made it very far when a light shines behind me. The man is following me in his car. He pulls up beside me, almost pinning me to the bank, the passenger-side window open, and I see him leaning toward me.

"Get in," he says. "Tell me where to go, and I'll take you to get help."

I look back, but can no longer see the family car. I feel trapped between the snowbank on the right and the car to my left. I know I can scurry below his bumper and keep going, but I don't. I'm tired and hungry, and I don't want to walk this road. I have seen scarier men.

I open the door and get into his car.

"Stay on Highway Two until you see the ranger station," I tell him.

He drives slowly, and I look out the window. I leave the

door unlocked and keep my hand on the handle, knowing I can roll out of a moving car. We've practiced this.

We drive a couple of miles in the dark, as the snow falls on the windshield, and he slows down as we approach the empty station.

"Now what?" he says.

I tell him he won't be able to drive up the dirt road, so he'll have to drop me off here. He stops the car and leaves the engine on. I open the door to leave, and as he grabs my arm, I instinctively cower, waiting for the blow.

"Are you sure you'll be okay out there?" he says warmly. "Do you know where you're going in the dark?"

I could navigate by the stars if they were visible. But even in this storm, where I can see only a foot or two ahead of me, I am not worried.

"I know where I'm going," I tell him. "Thank you for the ride."

As he drives away, he yells, "I'll call Highway Patrol at the next stop, just to make sure you get help."

But I don't respond. I am walking up a road I know so well I could find my way blindfolded or backward, with my hands tied. The snow is soft, and now that I am off the highway, it is noticeably higher. I sink to my knees with every step. My feet and ankles are numb, but I can feel the burn on my calves and thighs as I make my way up the mountain.

I know snow isn't good hydration, so I pick leaves of yerba santa that grow on the side of the road, and suck on them to relieve my thirst. Mother taught us that our bodies work harder to create the heat necessary to melt snow into a hydrating liquid, meaning you'll lose more water than you're taking in if you eat it. The only way to use snow for survival is if you have the tools necessary to melt it.

As I turn the final bend, I see the light of the mess hall, and I feel momentarily hopeful, until I am battered in the face by a snowball. It is rock-hard, and I reach up to feel my face begin to swell. "It's a girl!" someone yells, and the anonymous boys who have mistaken me for their opponent run away, afraid of remonstration from a leader who is sure to find out.

I want to cry, but I don't. I trudge up the last hill, enter the mess hall, and speak to the nearest leader, a man I have known since birth. He says Mr. Dowd has gone down to get wood, but he will go tell him what has happened, and I should warm up and wait. One of the younger leaders steps up and guides me to the large metal heater in the corner and brings me a cup of warm water. I hear the World War II–era Kaiser Willys Jeep start up. It has a plow attached. I assume Dad is on his way to pick up Mother and my siblings and transport them up the hill, so I take off my shoes and remove my dripping socks.

I wait. It takes a long time. Probably they are stuck. I take off my jacket and shake myself like an animal, flinging water from my hair. Boys begin to circle and stare at me. They aren't allowed to talk to a girl, so I lower my eyes and shiver as I begin to thaw.

Eventually, the heat kicks in, I stop shaking, and I sit in the corner and watch the boys play Bible Basketball, a boisterous game with five players on each team. They sit across from each other while a leader asks them questions, passing the answers like a ball between them, from center to the hoop on either side of the imaginary court. Then I hear shouting, and the boys around me scatter.

"What are you still doing here? Look at me. I'm talking to you! Do you hear me?" Dad is standing in the middle of the room, taller than the rest. It takes me a moment to realize his anger is directed at me.

Dad is in my face now. "Look at you. You should be ashamed of yourself!"

I fumble, trying to gather my shoes and coat.

"Get going girl, you hear me? Now!"

He grabs my wet shoulder so hard it will leave a bruise. "Get down to the house!"

I reach for my shoes, but he backhands me in the face before I can grab them. "I said, get to the house!"

I still have difficulty thinking the house the boys have built us is our home now, but I run there from the mess hall, barefoot in the snow. The rest of my family isn't there yet. Dad must be on his way to get them only now. I head straight to the bathroom, because there is a space heater there. I close the door and crawl into the corner and wait.

The house is quiet until I hear the Jeep again. As my family enters, I cower against the sounds they make, my breathing so fast and shallow I think I will pass out.

Mother enters the bathroom without knocking and turns on the bathtub faucet before she speaks. She looks at me like I am a wild animal and doesn't touch me. She must notice my swollen face, but she doesn't mention it. She extends a brown paper sack.

I take it from her and open it. It's empty.

"Put it over your mouth," she says. "Breathe into it."

I breathe into the bag and remove it to exhale.

"Keep it there," she whispers. "Breathe in and out through the bag."

I breathe in and out through the bag. I feel dizzy, but I keep going. She watches me until my breath slows.

Mother doesn't thank me for going on ahead, and she doesn't apologize for Dad's violence. Like all of these incidents, I know we won't speak of them again.

She turns off the water. "Get in, and keep breathing into the bag."

She leaves. I wait until I hear her footsteps recede before I peel off my wet clothes. I can't recall the last time she has seen me naked. It must have been when I was too young to remember.

I climb into the water, so hot I think it will scorch me. I reach for the bag. I keep my arms high to keep it from getting wet. I breathe in and breathe out. I try not to notice my breasts poking above the water. Mother has not yet mentioned binding, though that will come soon.

The water begins to cool. I sit in the tub with the paper bag, breathing in and out until I stop shivering and my breath calms.

Mother doesn't come back to check on me, so I make my way to bed with the bag. She has given me a new tool. And I will use it.

Jeffrey Pine

The Jeffrey pine is the most common tree in the Angeles National Forest, where it grows above 5,500 feet elevation and often hybridizes with ponderosa and Coulter pines. It grows 60 to 180 feet in height, and its bark is reddish brown, with a sweet odor similar to vanilla or pineapple, which can be sniffed in the cracks of the trees, particularly on warm days. Its needles are gray green and grow in threes, 4 to 9 inches long, with 6- to 10-inch-long cones, a flattened base, and curved, prickly scales.

    If you know what you're doing, you can live from Jeffrey pines for a long time, eating the needles, bark, pollen, and seeds. Any time of year, you can harvest the soft inner bark of the tree or make a tea from its needles. To obtain the bark, use a knife or a strong stick to dig in past the outer bark to find the tender white meat underneath. You can eat this raw or roast it over a campfire.

In late spring, you can harvest pine pollen from the male cones, which are smaller and softer than female cones and don't have rigid scales. When you tap them against your palm, they will release a light-yellow powder, containing 18 amino acids, minerals, vitamins, antioxidants, and enzymes. You can lick it off your hands or roll and shake the cones into a container, to collect and store the pollen.

To make tea, gather a handful of pine needles and break them up into the smallest possible pieces. Drop those pieces into a cup of boiling water and let them steep for several minutes, until the water turns a yellow-green color. Strain out the needles and drink.

Almost all pines have edible seeds, but the size and quality of those seeds depend on the species of pine tree. To collect the seeds, also called pine nuts, scour the ground for pine cones, particularly in the early fall, when the cones are dry and open. Once you have a pile of cones, look between the scales for little paper wings. When you gently pull out the wings, you'll see that there are pine nuts attached. You can bite them off and eat them raw.

OUR MOTHER LETS US WANDER anywhere we want on the Mountain, and has since the moment we got here. She doesn't restrict where we go, nor ask us what time we will return, but she does tell us what to do if we run into trouble.

Never put your hands or feet anywhere you can't see. If you need to step over a log, step up on it, look, then step down.

She tells us to watch for rattlesnakes and that when we encounter an animal that can hurt us, our options are: fight, flight, or freeze.

Apex predators are omnivores and have lots of options. If they surmise you'll put up a fight, they'll likely opt for smaller prey. But if you encounter a black bear, don't look it in the eye. Just back away slowly. If you encounter a brown bear, roll up in a ball. Either way, don't be afraid, our mother says. Be competent.

I think of the way Mother freezes around Dad, acting confident and unaffected when his anger flares. When the predator is significantly bigger than we are, we know not to fight or run. This will reduce the severity of injury.

What she teaches her daughters is different from what boys are taught at the Field, so we're not allowed to talk about what we know. The boys are taught to demonstrate physical superiority, to vie for it, to pummel one another in tackle football practice, which they are all required to play, starting at age five, getting accustomed to taking pain and being in the sun without water. They practice domination when social bonding, like sucker-punching each other or kicking one another's legs out from behind. They strap their gear and sleeping bags on their backs for long hikes and bike rides, sometimes going all the way from the Field up to the

Mountain, which is more than seventy-five miles of roads. They also chicken-fight on the field and in lakes, play Snake in the Grass and King of the Mountain, and have snowball fights and rubber-band gun wars. And they are all required to fight one another in boxing matches, which are part of tournaments, so you always know whom you're pitted against and who's the toughest.

Being tough for a girl is different. We spend long days enduring the abuse of boys, but the way Mother navigates this mountain is like the way she flows through the gauntlet of Grandpa and her brothers' cruelty and their insistence on her silence. In all terrain, Mother moves like water.

I want to be like water, because water is strong enough to wear down anything, and other than air, water is the most important thing for humans to have. You can live weeks without food, but you can't live long without water, especially in hot areas, where you'll lose large quantities of valuable water daily, sweating. Even in cold areas, your body needs two quarts of water daily to maintain efficiency. But you can get most of that from plants, if you know which ones to eat.

Just in case we get lost and don't make it back for the night, my sisters and I repeat back to our mother, "Survive fear. Survive with faith," which helps us remember shelter, fire, signaling, water, food. We know if we find ourselves stranded, we should attend to our needs in that particular order.

Our part of the Mountain may be only sixteen acres, but we are surrounded by US Forest Service land on all sides. And somewhere out there are more camps, though I've never seen one. We know the boundaries of our mountain, and we know where we're supposed to stop, although no one ever checks to make sure we do. We can easily wade through the pine needles to walk up the gully from the lower camp to the campfire ring, then on through the remnants of the upper camp to the chapel, and then up to the water tower, and then to a road. Beyond that, I don't know what there is. The trees appear to be endless.

No matter how far I go, I feel safe on this mountain, where I know the shape of the landscape, where my feet know the shape of the hills, where the ground is always firm beneath me. I feel safe here because the rules in nature are simple, because plants and animals do what their instincts tell them to and we know what to expect from them.

I never knew what to expect when we lived in the valley.

Before we came to the Mountain, the four of us kids shared a bedroom in a little house bordering a city dump in El Monte, a suburb east of Los Angeles. Mother let lots of stray animals live with us, and dogs often gave birth inside our bedroom closet. We watched the puppies bundle together in a cardboard box as the mother dog would come and go, nursing them when they cried. In a few weeks, she would wean her puppies, pushing them away when they tried to attach to her teats, and Mother would give the puppies to anyone who wanted one. They would cry and yelp at parting, but she didn't flinch.

When I asked her if she cared what happened to them next, she seemed surprised by the question. "They're dogs," she said. "They know how to take care of themselves."

Our parents were gone a lot when we were little, on the Trip, aimed at saving Outsiders. Sometimes they would sleep on the dirt in San Felipe, Mexico, where Grandma insisted on being a missionary. Sometimes we would go with them, living in tents for weeks at a time. Sometimes we stayed with whichever Field families had room, although each of us children was placed in a different home, so as not to outwear our welcome.

The best part of living in the valley was getting to go to school. Our parents didn't believe in secular school and said we weren't allowed to make friends there, but there was a public elementary school close to the Field, so we enrolled and walked there and back on our own. In the early days, our parents put up with this and seemed relieved we had somewhere else to be.

I tested into a program called Mentally Gifted Minors, so on the days when I stayed after school for the MGM program, I walked back to the Field alone. Mother seemed embarrassed by my participation, but she didn't ask me to stop going. The other kids in MGM didn't appear to be ashamed to be there; they seemed to enjoy playing chess and solving puzzles. But no matter how awesome these kids thought being gifted was, I hated being singled out.

In MGM, we didn't learn the kinds of things we did in the main classroom. The students were mixed ages, a couple per grade, which was supposed to help us make connections. Connections between numbers and shapes and spaces, and between letters and words, but also between one another and within ourselves.

A man led us, but he didn't call himself a teacher. He called himself a mentor, something he explained to us in a way we understood to mean we could talk about whatever we wanted and ask questions about anything. He wore shorts and moved around a lot and encouraged us to move around, so it felt more like PE than book learning and most of the kids took to calling him Coach. I didn't, because I was used to coaches who yell at you and tell you what to do.

Sometimes he took us on field trips, but always on foot, and he asked us what we noticed along the way.

One of the projects we worked on was mapmaking. We started with a map of the school, drawing the buildings and the classrooms and the grass and the walkways, but he also asked us to draw the things we noticed that other people might not, like where the kids play when teachers aren't looking, or other places the community was centered. He showed us maps of our city and state and country and world, and told us whatever was in the center is what the community thinks is important.

Some of the MGM kids drew monkey bars, some basketball or hopscotch courts, and some the cafeteria or vending machines. I drew flowers and weeds. Our mentor asked me about this, and when I told him I thought they were a part of the community, he asked me more questions and he listened to what I said. He helped us construct a map of our homes, even though he'd never seen them and we didn't bring in pictures. He said we could find what's important inside of us and put that at the center.

When I was seven and Lizbeth was eight, Becca was five, and Danny was three, we didn't have enough money to keep living in El Monte, so we had to leave. But I'd learned that *it is easier for a camel to go through the eye of a needle, than for a rich man to enter into the kingdom of God,* so I knew it was good to live without money.

Secretly, though, I wanted to make money instead of begging for it. In our family, we relied on God to clothe us like the lilies of the field, which mostly He did through tithes and other donations people gave to the Field when we told them that the end of the world was nigh and they should repent. When we didn't have enough to eat, that was God's plan too, because we were told, *Blessed are the poor.* And even when our faith was tried, we believed that God knew what he was doing and we had to trust that, because *There is a way which seemeth right unto a man, but the end thereof are the ways of death.*

That was all before we came to the Mountain. Like most things in our world, the path to get here was circuitous and never explained. We packed up all our belongings at our home in El Monte, along with our favorite dog Duchess. We left behind our short and only stint in a real school, moved into Grandpa's camper, which was called the Monitor, and hit the road, even though we didn't know where we were going.

Our parents and Danny slept in the Monitor, but during the months we spent traipsing together around the country, my sisters and I slept in tents, along with dozens of Grandpa's other followers. On this instance of the Trip, with our larger Field family, we all performed in a musical about how all things are possible with God, if you believe. We went on the

Trip many times, before and after we moved to the Mountain, but this one is the most memorable, because of a fire. It was the fire that made us make the Mountain our home.

But I'm getting ahead of myself. The Trip is how Grandpa culls his followers and makes them into disciples. Whenever we are on the Trip, we stick to a precise routine, doing everything in the same order, the same way, no matter where we are.

As girls, we wear identical clothes hand-sewn by godly women, so that we always know who is in our group. The boys wear collared shirts and slacks, or suits for important events. As girls, we wear pastel colors, in soft patterns of swirls, which make us look accommodating and nonthreatening.

We keep our personal items in bins under the bus, except our Bibles, which we keep inside the bus, because as we drive, Grandpa gives devotions, speaking to us all for hours at a time with a microphone he wears around his head. When Grandpa is speaking, we must keep our eyes on him at all times.

One time, when Danny was three, he started falling asleep in the aisle and Grandpa kicked him in the head with his big black shoe to wake him up. Grandpa may have been a prophet, but that was the first time I knew he would never be my god.

On the Trip, everything we do is liturgical, and we all memorize many verses, so we can speak to one another as if we are continually in covenant. On the Trip, we work together as a unit, with no concern for our individual needs.

In some ways, it's not that different from living on this mountain. In other ways, it is.

At night, in the campgrounds, we wear djellabas, to keep men from looking at our bodies. A djellaba is a long robe with a large hood that covers everything but your face, including your hands and feet. Mine had stripes of many colors, and I felt proud to wear it, like Joseph, whose father loved him best *and made him a coat of many colors.* I wore it every day until it burned up in the fire.

But I don't miss it that much. It was really long and hard not to stumble over, and it was difficult to ever see anything around me under that big hood. But we don't wear djellabas on the Mountain, because the only boys who come up here are the boys from the Field, and they know better than to look at girls. At least when anyone is watching.

While we were traveling through the southern states in the Monitor, putting on our proselytizing plays, Mother first taught us if a man approached us and held us captive, we weren't supposed to scream.

Don't draw attention to yourself, girls. And don't put up a fight.

She told us to do whatever the man told us to do, for *blessed are the meek,* but also we should keep our eyes open and look around until we find a camper where old people are staying. We should be kind to the man who has captured us, so that he won't have to restrain us or put a bag over our heads. Mother told us a man might try to drag us to his car, but that we should go willingly, so that he wouldn't have to grip us harder or use his knife or gun to subdue us.

Make sure you can always look around, girls.

I didn't know how we were supposed to do that in djellabas.

But the point is, if a dangerous man is dragging you, you should look for old people in a campsite and then pretend those people are your people and call out to them like they're family. Mother also says that if you rejoice and reach up to hug and thank a man for escorting you, it will catch him off guard, and then you can glide out of his arms and find safety.

She says this will work because she heard on the news about a woman who escaped her own rape, death, and dismemberment in a parking garage through this very strategy.

"You know," Mother tells us, "this young woman was walking briskly to her car in a dark parking garage after work one evening, with her keys pushed against the webbing of two fingers—you should learn this, girls, so you can stab an assailant—when a large man approached her from behind and wrapped an arm firm around her waist, pressing her tight to his crotch, and put a hand over her mouth, so she couldn't scream. She couldn't see him, of course, but she knew what he wanted as he began to push her toward his car."

I picture myself being dragged to a car by my braids, the hand over my mouth gloved so I can't hurt him with my bites.

"But this girl was clever," Mother says. "She turned around and hugged him, saying, 'I'm sooooooo glad you're here, darling! You scared the living daylights out of me, you crazy man, you!' And she kissed him on the cheek, like she meant it. With the gentleness of her affection, the man loosened his grip, but she continued to play her little game.

'Darling, I'm such an idiot. I left my lipstick in the bathroom. Let me just pop in and grab it before we go. I want to look pretty for you.' And of course, she ran into the building and didn't come out. The man went on to rape and dismember other women, but not her, and that ability to keep her wits about her during an assault saved her life."

"Wouldn't that be hard to do when you're scared?" I once asked Mother.

"A lot of things are hard about being a woman," she said, "but that's our lot in life. You've got to be smarter than your predators, but don't let them know it."

When the men in our family scared me, I practiced acting overjoyed. And if I saw a threatening man on the Outside, I smiled at him too, just in case.

One day, when we were traveling through Indiana, the Monitor caught fire. Danny was three years old and asleep in the back with our dog Duchess, because Mother didn't like having Danny in the bus causing a ruckus, the way little kids do.

We were riding in the bus with the other followers; Dad was driving the bus, and Mother was sitting in front, preaching devotions. We were in a line of vehicles the Field used on the Trip, moving along the highways like a funeral procession. A woman was driving the Monitor when the gas tank underneath came unhinged, scraped along the bottom of the road, and caught on fire.

The woman pulled Danny out before the entire vehicle burst into flames, but Grandpa never let a woman drive a vehicle again. He didn't say anything about Duchess, who burned up along with all our things, because we weren't supposed to care about that.

We stayed on the Trip with the rest of the followers, but when it ended, we had nowhere else to go. Grandpa was tired of us living with him, so we moved up to the Mountain to get back on our feet.

Some family members think we deserved what happened to us, because we aren't as pure as Grandpa says we should be. But I don't pay them much mind.

Blessed are ye, when men shall revile you, and persecute you, and shall say all manner of evil against you falsely, for my sake.

When I ask Lizbeth why God punished Duchess for our sins, she says, "She's just a dog. It's not the same as if one of us burned up."

So I ask Mother to explain it to me, and she whispers, "Hush now. Your brother got out and didn't burn up with Duchess, so be grateful, and don't look back, lest the Lord turn you into a pillar of salt."

Becca and I give each other looks, but not sad ones, because we don't want to make each other cry.

It's very important not to cry. Grandpa says we have to be tough to lead in the army of God, and Mother and Dad insist that means no crying, not ever, because John *saw an angel come down from heaven, having the key of the bottomless pit and a great chain in his hand. And he laid hold on the dragon, that old serpent, which is the Devil, and Satan, and bound him a thousand years, and cast him into the bottomless pit, and shut him up, and set a seal upon him, that he*

should deceive the nations no more, till the thousand years
should be fulfilled: and after that he must be loosed a little
season.

Outsiders don't study this, but we do, so we can be prepared. But prepared or not, we don't know when the trumpet will sound, signaling the end of the world as we know it and the beginning of the millennium, which is a thousand years of terror or peace, depending on who is doing the interpreting. Grandpa has been telling people that the Camp David Accords will determine this—when a peace treaty between Israel and Egypt will be signed or not signed—but until then, we just watch and wait.

Later, when Becca is seven, she will draw a picture of the fire, with Duchess burning up and Danny lying safe on the side of the road, curled up in a little ball, like a sleeping baby. Later, the woman who was driving the Monitor will frame this picture, and it will hang in her house for many years, and I will look at it every time I babysit her children.

But right now, sitting on a log on this mountain, remembering how we got here, losing our dog and all our belongings, even the near death of our brother feels ordinary, like any other bend in the road.

After Duchess and all of our things burned up, we got right back on the bus and continued the Trip as planned. I didn't have a toothbrush, or a comb for my hair, for the weeks it took us to get from Indiana to this mountain. I was embarrassed by my knotty hair, how the tangles built up in the back so much it was hard to even hide them inside my ponytail, but Lizbeth said we should accept things as they were, because that was God's plan for us. Lizbeth said that about everything, because she is a very good girl.

I remember what we were wearing that day, not just because those would be the only clothes I wore for a month, but also because Becca and Lizbeth were wearing the same clothes, so the pastel-blue pants and rainbow-patterned shirts are etched in my mind like the words we imprint on the letter-press we use for church bulletins. I don't tell Mother, but I hate everything about baby blue and won't wear it anymore, not since the fire, no matter what she says.

She didn't tell us what to wear next. Dad's mom, whom we call Grammie even though we don't know her—she moved back to the East Coast when Dad was eighteen—sent some money, and we each got to choose an outfit from the Sears catalog. Before we got to the Mountain, the clothes were waiting for us in a circular building made out of wood in a little town called Wrightwood. The woman who gave us our clothes smiled at us and said we could change there.

It smelled so good to be in new clothes that I wanted to stay with her and work and live there. She said I was too young for a job, but she gave me a catalog and said we could use it when we were ready to order more. She didn't know that our family didn't have the money to order clothes, but I didn't tell her that and I took it anyway, because I'm not a very good girl.

The catalog has 1,528 pages and describes all the clothes anyone could ever imagine, and undergarments I will have to wear one day too. There are so many words in this catalog, more words than I have ever owned, except maybe for the

Bible I got when I was six, but that burned up in the fire, so I can't conduct an accurate comparison. I don't tell anyone that I kept the catalog, or that I read every word of it. Mother wouldn't approve.

When we first arrive on the Mountain, it looks big and scary, but not as big or scary as the road we have been traveling on or the dangerous men all along it. I am turning eight, and I think I may be home.

Our mother uses a knife to scrape out the last of our peanut butter and massages it into the holes of a pine cone. She dips the pine cone in birdseed and hangs it from the tree in front of the mess hall. She says the birds talk to the trees, and the trees talk to one another, in ways we don't understand.

She says we will learn to name all the birds and all the trees. Then she lets us into the mess hall, a big room that was built long before we were born. She says we will stay here until we can build a house, and she shows us our bunks. The room is full of old army cots the boys use when they come up here for camp to learn about God. Mother says we can sleep anywhere we want. I secure a spot on top, near the big window, so that I can see the world.

I hide my Sears catalog under my mattress.

She sets army mats on the floor for her and our father, and she presses them together and covers them with sheets and blankets, like a little nest. Seeing this, I want to be on the floor too, safe like they get to be, where maybe you can have bad dreams and not worry about falling off onto the concrete. I tell our parents we should all sleep on the floor, but they say no, and they don't let us push the bunks together either. We're never allowed to cuddle with one another.

We get used to walking down the hill to the outhouse at night, but Danny doesn't want to. Lizbeth and Becca complain about the dirt and the cold and the smell, but Danny just freezes up and refuses to go in. When he wets his pants, our parents get furious. So I hold his hand and take him with me. I stand outside the outhouse, trying to coax him in. He says he is afraid of falling down the hole.

I think of that dark hole, with all the layers of human filth, and I wonder if that's what hell is like: a place of human filth, where there is weeping and gnashing of teeth.

From then on, I take my brother bush hunting when our parents aren't looking. I tell them we are learning to hike, and I go out and stand with him under the night sky so that he will be less afraid of the man in the moon, who our mother says watches us and reports back to God. I tell Danny that I know this man, and I will distract him while he does his business.

And so I begin conversations with the man in the moon, and I look up and tell stories about what this man thinks, how he gets lonely, how sometimes he dances with the hunter Orion. Or how when he's thirsty, he drinks from the Big Dipper, how he laughs at the Great Dog, how if we listen closely enough, we can hear him play the harp.

I want to remember them, so I write these little stories in verse, like a psalm, in the margins of the Sears catalog I hide under the mattress.

Mother tells us to bring in the acorns from the tree out front. We take off their hats and play with them, creating little groups, like they are our friends. Sometimes we draw faces on them, until Mother tells us to stop being ridiculous and hand them over for cooking. She piles all of our collections into one big, steaming pot and boils them until they are safe to eat. We lay them out to dry for three days, and then we crack some of the soft shells and eat the meat inside with salt. Some, we pound into flour. Later, we will add water to that and flip them into something that tastes a little like pancakes.

We have been living on the Mountain for three months when the day before Christmas rolls around. I know I should be most excited to celebrate baby Jesus, who came to earth to die for my sins, but I am most excited by the snow. The snow is whiter than anything I have ever seen.

In the morning, I go down to the outhouse, where the animal tracks look like someone has made imprints for casts. The sun shines down on us, and everything around glitters. It's not just shining, like they say in songs, but it looks like someone actually dropped a whole bottle of glitter on it. It reminds me of a hymn, which I sing as I hike down the hill: "Lord, wash me, and I shall be whiter than snow. Whiter than snow, yes, whiter than snow. Lord, wash me, and I shall be whiter than snow."

There is another storm coming, so we can't drive down the hill to the Field for the Christmas Eve service. My siblings and I are struck silent and still by the prospect of being confined, although we don't think to call it that. We are huddled at the top of a dirt road, safe in the mess hall, relieved that it is impossible to make the long trek down to Grandpa's Communion.

We talk about the baby Jesus and snack on the pine seeds we have been collecting all week.

I ask Mother what having a baby is like, but she won't answer. Lizbeth nudges me to ask again, to find out if mothers love their babies more than anything, and I whisper back to her that she should ask.

She says, "No, you," and we go back and forth like that a little, because children should be seen and not heard, and Lizbeth doesn't like to get in trouble.

Mother doesn't like when we ask her the same question she refused to answer the first time, and I tell Lizbeth, "Wait. I'll think of a better way to ask that."

Mother thinks we are fighting and tells us to stop. "You know what Solomon did when two mothers both claimed the same baby was theirs, right?"

I know this story, but we all shake our heads, so that she'll keep telling it.

"Well, in those days, when people lived closer together in tribes, women slept with their babies. One of the mothers rolled over on her baby and killed it during the night. She was distraught when she woke up and found her baby dead, so she swapped her dead baby with another mother's live one, and when that mother woke up and found her baby dead, she shrieked out in anguish. But then she recognized that the dead baby wasn't hers, and she challenged the woman who had her baby to give it back. The woman claimed the baby was hers and wouldn't relent. Both women were adamant the baby was theirs, and there was no resolution to their bickering. So eventually, servants took the women and the baby to King Solomon to make a final judgment. Solomon raised the baby up and said, 'Since you can't agree, we will cut the baby in half and give each of you half.' The fake mother said nothing, but of course the real mother cried out, 'No, she can have the baby.' And Solomon said, 'Give the baby to the real mother. Only a real mother would rather have her child alive in someone else's hands than dead in her own.'"

I love when Mother tells us stories, even if they're from the Bible, and even if I've heard them before, which I pretty much always have. I feel like the luckiest girl in the world to be in this winter wonderland, away from the possibility that our parents will be summoned to coach or preach or teach. I don't want anything for Christmas except to stay here forever, to stop driving down the hill, to never have to leave the Mountain again, for this cocooning to never end.

We are fortunate that there is a huge stone fireplace next to the kitchen, where we can dry our wet things and hang stockings. We have felt stockings, with felt images, pieced together by women who have been called by the Lord to work with their hands. I wish I would find jewelry in my stocking tomorrow, but I know Santa isn't real and Mother doesn't want me to care about appearances.

Our parents rustle in together after visiting the outhouse, and Dad tells us to get ourselves up onto our cots. After a while, Mother pulls out her violin and begins to play "I Need Thee Every Hour."

Mother still has her violin. She left it at the Field during the Trip, so it didn't burn up in the Monitor. Now she is playing "How Great Thou Art."

I look out at the nearly full moon, and its reflection on the snow is so bright that through the big window, I can see the sleeping faces of my sisters, their hands under their cheeks, looking like they're righteous.

Mother moves on to "Are You Washed in the Blood," and I picture a red snow plant, peeking its head up in the spring. She has been preparing these songs for the past couple of nights, because she always plays her violin at Grandpa's Christmas Eve Communion ceremony.

Grandma used to accompany her on the piano, before she had her stroke. Mother and Grandma would play hymns while Grandpa gave us the body and blood of Christ. Grandpa always takes his time, touching the forehead of each of his followers, whispering and chanting to each one of them, so Mother has to have a lot of hymns prepared.

When I was little, Grandma taught me to sing soprano while she sang alto. She taught me to play all the major keys on the piano, and we were starting to make the shifts back and forth through minor, augmented, and diminished.

Since her stroke, I've been wanting to teach them back to her, but we don't get to see her very often, now that we live on the Mountain. "A Mighty Fortress Is Our God." I move my fingers, like I'm playing the piano on my sleeping bag. "Leaning on the Everlasting Arms." "Bringing In the Sheaves." My fingers curl to play the chords. "Amazing Grace." "Great Is Thy Faithfulness."

The night in our bunks is cold, and although we shiver, we are full of hope. Mother's music sounds like singing. She doesn't like when I make comparisons like that. If I told her the violin sounds like a voice, she would tell me I'm fabricating. She says fabricating is a sin, so now I do it only in my head.

Now her violin sounds like a duet with dissonance. I have to remember to write that down in the margins of the Sears catalog, where I've started keeping all my favorite lines, going back to them over and over when no one is looking.

"The man in the moon is watching us, Danny," I whisper, knowing the sound of the music will muffle my words. My brother's face is glowing from the moonlight, and he looks over at me with droopy eyes, like he's been ordered to nod off but refuses.

"Is that God?" he asks. "Is that where God lives? Or Santa Claus?"

"God lives in heaven," I say. "Santa lives at the North Pole."

"Is the North Pole on earth or in heaven?"

"The North Pole is where the magic happens on earth. God saves *his* magic for after we die."

"I don't want you to die."

I look at Danny with maternal confidence, like I know what I'm talking about. "Santa won't let me die tonight. But if I do, if I die before you, I will ask God to make sure Santa takes extra good care of you."

"Lights out," our father barks, and darkness descends as if from the hand of God.

WE WAKE UP. Underneath the stockings are four suitcases: yellow for Lizbeth, pink for me, blue for Becca, and brown for Danny. We will live out of these suitcases for the next ten years.

Yucca

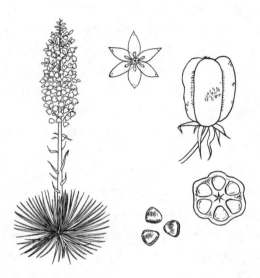

Yucca is a shrublike plant with a single stem or a few short stems surrounded by narrow stiff leaves at the expanded base. Its flowers, which each have three petals, grow on a central stalk. Its fruit, which follows the flower, is fleshy and approximately 6 or 7 inches long, resembling a short banana.

Commonly referred to as "our Lord's candle," yucca can be found on dry slopes from 3,000 to 6,000 feet elevation.

All parts of the yucca can be useful to humans, and as it matures throughout the year, different sections of the plant become edible. Prior to blooming, you can cut the flower stalk and cook it overnight to soften it. You can also eat the

young flowers, though if you're new to this, you'll want to
boil and purge the cooking water multiple times, to eliminate
the sharp taste.

The fruits can be eaten raw or roasted. The seeds can
be consumed whole or pounded into a paste. The heart of
a yucca plant and the stalk of the flower spike can both be
roasted or boiled on an open fire pit and eaten like squash.

MOTHER DOESN'T LIKE WHEN WE TALK. But sometimes
when we're out on training trips, she tells us stories, and
that's almost like a conversation.

I like the intensity of training trips, even though it's
unclear what the end of the world we're training for will look
like. Unlike the Trip, these training trips are sporadic and
unplanned, so I don't get to look forward to them as much
as I would like. I guess that is kind of the point, though. We
should be ready for anything, for *the day of the Lord will*
come as a thief in the night.

Sometimes we hike long distances on these training trips,
and sometimes we ride in the back of the World War II–era
Jeep that Dad picked up from government surplus. Mother
says you have to go where you can to get what you need. Even
when you don't know where you're going.

Today we take the Jeep, because we are collecting boulders
to build an irrigation system. We head out to the high desert,
about fifteen miles east on the 138, toward Mormon Rocks,
a region in the Mojave Desert with a nearly endless supply
of stones, some of which will be the sizes we need. Mother

brings the transistor radio and a walkie-talkie, in case Ranger Harold from the Forest Service needs to reach her.

On this warm spring day, while we heave rocks into the back of the Jeep, Mother tells us that these sandstone formations should really be called Serrano Rocks, because the Serrano people lived here long before the Mormons came through. She says it's a shame they don't teach real history in the schools these days. "Many Native peoples lived in these caverns for thousands of years as hunter-gatherers. We just don't know who they were."

"How do we know about the Serrano?" I ask.

"Because they're the most recent. We know they lived here for at least seven hundred years before the Mormons came through in the 1840s. There was a massacre here during Civil War times, although people don't talk about that much. Can't blame the desert Indians for not wanting to give up the last of what was theirs, can you? No one teaches you that in those useless public schools, but what happened here was its own civil war, between how people lived on this land for centuries and what the Europeans who came through mandated it become. In the mid-nineteenth century, the Mormons didn't take favorably to the Serrano or to any of the Native tribes. I mean, they said they were okay with peaceful Indians, but who could be peaceful when someone comes in and takes away your way of life?"

Mother keeps lifting rocks this whole time while she's talking, but even when she gets riled up, her breath stays steady.

"But you know they're still here, the Indians," she says.

"Mostly on reservations, where white people can keep them under control."

Mother knows a lot about things they don't teach in school, and unlike Grandpa, she's adamantly against keeping people confined.

"Your dad plays basketball with the Sherman Indians, you know, so you should ask him sometime what they say about all this."

I look at her, not sure I've heard her correctly. I can't imagine Dad talking about this. Dad doesn't talk about anything except military training. I guess I don't know what Dad does in the weeks and months he's not with us. But whatever I've been imagining him doing has never included playing basketball with Indians—I can tell you that.

I file this information away to ponder later. All I can think about right now is how hungry I am. Were the Serrano hungry out here, when the only food they had was what the desert offered? The high desert is a tough place to forage, but Mother says everywhere on earth, there is life, so there is always sustenance if you know how to look for it.

Training in the desert prepares us for the trials and tribulations to come, which John predicted in Revelation through lots of symbols, many of which we've memorized, so we'll have the muscle memory to respond effectively.

I think about the Mormons, and what they ate along the trail they carved here a century ago. Why did they come here? It couldn't be because they wanted access to the Serranos' food. It's not easy living off the food you can find here. Most white people don't have the patience for the work it takes to forage in regions they don't understand. The Mormons must have brought their own beef jerky or cornmeal mush or salt-rising bread. There is no way they relied on yucca and prickly pear cacti, or getting water from distilling urine in a pit, like Mother taught us to do.

I look at the yucca, yellow and flowering and abundant across the landscape, which makes everything look like a fairyland. Mother says we are in luck. She says you'll never go hungry in the spring out here.

She tells us, "Where there is color, there is nourishment. If you can see color, you have access to nature's dance, and following her rhythm will help you find the bread crumbs you need to survive."

When Mother talks about bread crumbs, she means metaphorically. We never pack food on these trips. We just eat what we find along the way, because Jesus said his disciples needed nothing when they went out to preach his word: no bag, no bread, no copper in their money belts.

Mother says most people boil yucca flowers before eating them, but when the petals are young and soft, you don't need to, and you should never count on having enough water to waste on cooking; one of the best things about yucca flowers is the embedded moisture, so take it as a gift and don't mess with it. Plus, she says it's good to get used to raw plant fiber, so your body won't rebel if you have to rely on it.

She tells us the Serrano call yucca "holy weed," because of its many uses, like fire kindling, rope, sandals, cloth, and soap, almost like a general store.

"Isn't yerba santa the holy weed?" I ask.

"According to the Spanish, but you know, Indians had their own forms of holy and their own languages of worship. But," she admonishes us in advance, "*you* shouldn't call it 'holy weed.' That's not our language. We call it 'our Lord's candle.' Remember that."

Before we eat, she wants to show us something. As she peels back the outer layer of the yucca flower, she points to a moth living inside the seed pods.

"There are four kinds of yucca moths, each adapted for one species of yucca," she explains. "The female moth gathers pollen from a flower, rolls it up and takes it to another flower. She then lays a few eggs inside the flower and inserts the pollen. The pollinated yucca flower becomes a pod filled with seeds, which the moth larvae eat before becoming moths. The larvae eat about half of the eggs a yucca plant produces. Neither the yucca plant nor the yucca moth can exist without the other. No other insect pollinates the yucca plant, nor does the yucca moth pollinate any other plant. They are dependent on each other for their existence, which is called mutualism."

Mother encourages us to eat. Lizbeth nudges me and whispers, "Are there any larvae in these flowers?"

I shrug. "Why don't you ask Mother?"

"You ask her."

Usually, I'll acquiesce, but this question isn't worth it. Like many of the questions we ask other people, I already know the answer. In this case, I'm trying to protect Lizbeth from the knowledge of the larvae she will be consuming with the flowers, but I can't let on. Mother doesn't believe in protecting children from anything.

Plus, I know we are fortunate to have access to the larvae that live in the flowers, and that's part of the reason we eat them. Larvae provide a solid source of protein, which humans need. So I eat, without asking questions, and I feed Lizbeth as well, although I don't think she swallows.

We go back to our work, and I feel better already. I get lost in the rhythm of the rocks, hauling the ones I can lift, one by one, to the Jeep when Mother says she is taking the younger children toward Table Top Mountain to look at an owl that might need care. She tells Lizbeth and me we should continue collecting the rocks, so that we don't lose too much of the productive daylight while she's gone.

Lizbeth whispers to me, "Tell Mother you don't need me, that you'll be fine."

There are only certain fights with Lizbeth that are worth having. This isn't one of them.

I say what she wants me to say and I stay on, alone. Mother doesn't leave me with water or anything else out here, but the point of survival training isn't what supplies you can bring with you, but what you can live without.

I continue to lift rocks, building a pile for when they return.

I wish Lizbeth had stayed with me, and not just because I wish she liked me. Lizbeth hates to be alone and she's not very good at hiking, but she's really good at memorizing things. She is good at making the tools the way you're supposed to make them. She knows how to navigate geography, space, and time by the sun and the stars, using sticks and stones as mark posts. And Lizbeth knows Morse code. If we were ever captured, she would know how to blink out a message for rescue without our captors knowing.

I survey the landscape, observing things I didn't notice when we were in our family group. I think about what I will do if they don't come back.

Survive fear. Survive with faith.

- **Shelter** Location, location, location. Decide where you will build your nest. Choose a flat space on high ground (a large rock or a mound of dirt, where you can remove roots and debris), away from well-used animal trails, leaning trees, and snow or rockfall areas. A good shelter in a bad location is a bad shelter.

- **Fire** A fire can prevent you from freezing or keep you warm enough to do the other tasks you'll need to ensure your protection. Cooking can increase the range of food you can consume, keep away bugs and wild animals, and improve your overall sense of security. Consider site selection and site preparation away from your shelter. Without matches, your setup will be crucial. Before you attempt to start your fire, collect ample tinder, kindling, and fuel.

- **Signaling** Ask yourself: *Who knows I am missing? Is anyone looking for me? When is the earliest possible moment a search could begin? Do I want to be found?* If you want to be found, signal early and often. If the landscape on which you are stranded is dark, collect light rocks. If it's light, collect dark rocks. Find a clearing and spell out *SOS*. Make three small fire pits, designed for maximum smoke. If you hear a plane, you will rush to light them. If there is no clearing, use the brightest color fabric you have (tear it from your clothing, if that's your only option), and tie three flags to the highest tree you can climb.

- **Water** Dehydration will directly affect your ability to make logical decisions. Once you have built your shelter, home in on your water system. Water is the earth's blood, giving life to all the world's beings. Honor it. The blood in our veins, the sap in the trees, and the water of rivers and streams are united in shared sisterhood. If there is no running water, use a jacket or anything you may have that resembles plastic to build an evaporation net. Find a sunny spot near vegetation to dig a hole as wide as your plastic. Place a cup or anything you can improvise as a container inside the hole, and then cover your hole with the flat plastic, securing it around the perimeter with rocks. You will also need to place a rock on the center of the plastic, directly over the container. Condensation will collect in your container overnight, yielding up to a quart of water a day.

- **Food** If it could take more than a couple of weeks for someone to find you, or if you are running from something and want to remain hidden, you will need to

sustain your energy with food. Depending on the season during which you are stranded, this may be simple
or it may be difficult.

Mother will probably come back, eventually. If I feel hungry in the meantime, I can feed myself with yucca flowers
and larvae. If I walk a few hundred yards, I am certain I'll
find desert dandelions, which are even easier to consume. I
am comforted, knowing I have solid options.

But the truth is, we never know when Mother will be back.
Sometimes she is gone for months at a time. We have to trust
our training and believe in our own abilities. Some people
think plants appear in your life at the time you most need their
healing powers, and stay present for as long as you need them.
I want to believe this, but Mother says that's ridiculous.

Have a plan. Survive fear. Survive with faith. Because
faith without works is dead.

About an hour later, I am pleasantly surprised to hear the
sound of a vehicle, and I look up, relieved that the family has
come back so long before nightfall. When I lift my head, I
am startled to see a short bus approaching. My eyes can just
barely make out the writing on the bus: CALIFORNIA DEPART-
MENT OF CORRECTIONS AND REHABILITATION.

The bus parks a hundred yards from me, and boys in
jumpsuits file out and begin to rake up brush and bits of trash
strewn from the road.

I smile and wave, like I'm not scared. The boys don't wave
back, but Mother says be nice to people who scare you. Smile
at them. Hug them. Give them candy.

But if I'd had candy, I would already have eaten it.

I remember one day when one of the boys who lived with us tackled me, pushing me on my back and then sitting on my hips, pressing his hands against my shoulders so I couldn't get up, making me stay still while he licked my face.

I told Mother what happened, and she said I shouldn't have run when he chased me. "Men always chase you when you run," she says. Then she went into her room and shut the door.

I thought she was done with me and started to walk away, but she came back. "Here," she said, handing me a Snickers bar. "Give him this, and ask him to treat you like a lady."

I took the candy bar, intending to do as she instructed. But before I saw him again, I was hungry and I ate it.

The boys stay near the road, focusing on clearing potential fire hazards. Although this is my first time seeing them up close, Dad had told us we might run into "the Fenner boys" sometime on the mountain, since the California Youth Authority had recently partnered with Cal Fire, and the Fenner Canyon Conservation Camp is only a few miles from us, housing young men who need to repay society for things they've done wrong.

I don't have any candy out here, and no matter what Mother says about yucca flowers, they're not the same and they won't do the trick. But I'm not scared of the Fenner boys. There is a man with a gun in his holster who keeps them in line.

Eventually, Mother comes back with the other children, who hop out and help me load the rest of the rocks into the back of the Jeep. As darkness descends, Lizbeth gets in the front with Mother and the rest of us climb in the back of the Jeep with the boulders.

I assume we're going home, but we don't. We drive into the campground near Table Top Mountain, which is empty on weekdays. We step out into the night and follow Mother, climbing over logs into a gulch. She has brought along a tape recorder, which I am guessing we will use to record owl sounds, since I know for months now she has been out at night recording the various vocalizations of local owls.

During the days, we have been listening and relistening to her tapes, until we can identify whether the calls come from the commonly sighted great horned owl, or the less common spotted, flammulated, pygmy, or saw-whet owls, which all sound distinctly different. We have also learned to differentiate between the intonations of when they are calling to establish territories, cuing food sources, attracting mates, or signaling that there's a predator nearby.

As we settle into the gulch, I notice a lodgepole pine, and I know that if I needed to I could peel away the outer bark, strip noodles off the inner bark, and eat them raw. I rub my hand along the tree, thinking about where the best place to start would be. My hand is sticky from the resin, and I roll the pitch between my fingers into a little ball. You can chew on this when your throat is sore from thirst. I pop the wad into my mouth, like gum.

Mother reminds us about the night she brought a baby owl home in one of her many portable wire cages, and how she woke us up to sit with it. Up near this campground, a young great horned owl had left its nest too early, when it wasn't capable of flying. Some of the city folk campers were hassling it, and the rangers who had been called in to help didn't know what to do. So they contacted Mother on our CB radio to ask if she could intercede. She hiked up the hill and, wearing her sturdy gloves, scooped the owl into a cage and took him back home to keep him safe for the night.

We watched the young owl with curiosity, wanting to befriend it, but Mother admonished us not to touch him. "When humans touch what is wild, we interfere with the natural order of things," she said. "Go outside. Look around. But never touch wild things if you want them to thrive."

When the rangers arrived for duty the next day, Mother had already released the owl, and to keep them from interfering, she didn't tell them where.

I had hoped we could keep it, but Mother said owls aren't meant to be kept.

She says it's time to be quiet now, although she's the only one who has said a word since we got to the campground. I have already closed my eyes and burrowed into the dirt when I hear the click of the button on the tape recorder, and owl sounds fill the night. I open my eyes. We aren't recording. Tonight, she is playing one of her own owl tapes.

A great horned owl lands low in a tree right in front of us. We watch and listen as he *hoooo hooooo*s back and forth with the recording. We don't speak, but there's no need; we understand the conversation. The owl in our tree sits tight and hoots to establish the boundaries of its territory, kind of like we do at the Field.

The owl in the recording and our live owl take turns calling until the tape ends. Then the great horned owl flies away.

Mother doesn't move, so we don't move either. We sit quietly for a long time, listening to the whooshing of the wind. I suspect my sisters are asleep, but I am wide-awake, waiting for what will happen next.

Eventually, I hear a high-pitched beeping sound. A saw-whet owl alights in a tree to our left. I watch Mother slowly get up and move toward the tree. She has left the tape recorder and her flashlight behind, which means she plans to come back.

She crouches low and settles herself in at the trunk of the tree across from us, articulating her own little alarm sounds in sync with the owl. As he turns his head, I can see glimpses of his large yellow eyes glowing in the dark. The alarm sounds he is making don't seem to escalate in response to her presence.

After a while, still huddled next to the tree across from us, Mother says we can shine the flashlight into the tree. I reach for the light, letting my sisters sleep, more mesmerized by my duet with Mother than the fierce phosphorescence of the owl's eyes.

I turn off the flashlight, and his eyes still glow. Mother says they remind her of Ross's alligators down south, and I burrow into the gulch, eagerly anticipating her story, pretending she's bringing it out for me alone.

"I first met Ross Allen when we toured the Ross Allen Reptile Institute in Silver Springs, Florida," she says. "One of the girls wrote him a letter to see if we could meet with him next time we were out that way, and he wrote back and said yes. So we met him at his home, which was like a zoo. He had caged animals everywhere and an alligator pond with a small pier, and there were no side rails where we walked out to view them."

I can picture this perfectly, because I was there. She often doesn't remember which of her children were or weren't present on the Trip. This was one of the first times Grandpa let a group of girls go on the Trip, and of course he put Mother in charge of the girls' group.

"Then we followed him out on a hike with some of the girls from the Field who were on the Trip. As soon as we left his ranch, he took us to a stream and talked about the poisonous water moccasins that were there. I was right behind him when he told us that, and then he just turned around and started walking across that stream. He never looked back to see if we were coming, and I didn't know what to do.

"I decided I wasn't going to be left out there without him, so your father and I started crossing, even though he had leather shoes on. The girls in back must have decided to come too, because what else was there to do out there in the dark swamp with those alligators looming? Ross just kept hiking and we kept hiking with him, throughout the Everglades, and he kept telling us stories about everything.

"We came to a huge lake out there, and he taught us how to use our flashlights to look for the eyeshine of alligators. We spotted several out there, and then he pointed out one large one. While it was too dark to see him, he had the largest eyeshine, so I remember him well. Ross told us he wrestled him once, but we didn't get to watch him do that.

"We ended that evening with a campfire in the wilderness. Ross went out and picked herbs to make us tea, pouring it into the paper cups he brought for us in his pouch, and we sat around and listened to more stories. Around one in the morning, we headed back to his place."

I prefer the mountains to the swamps, listening to the saw-whet owl sounding its alarm into the blue-black night. There are no snakes I'm afraid of out here, and no alligators either.

I look at my siblings, asleep on the ground, and I am relieved it is only us, that there aren't more people Mother needs to guide tonight.

I picture us as Abraham's seeds, as indistinct to her as sands on the seashore or stars in the heavens. We aren't unique, like fingerprints, or sensuous, like the sounds she brings forth from her violin. When Mother comes and goes, leading God's people as she's called to do, she doesn't say goodbye or tell us when she'll be back. When she returns, we don't hear a hello, as if her heavy footprints leave no trace on our bodies or our hearts.

Mother doesn't believe in looking back, instead *forgetting those things which are behind, and reaching forth unto those things which are before.* Her departures are becoming more frequent, and they leave me with a hollowness I don't know how to fill. Parenting isn't her calling.

I strain to hear the sounds that summon her to *press toward the mark for the prize of the high calling of God in Christ Jesus,* but I don't know what to listen for. The only sound I know God and his angels make is on a trumpet, and I haven't heard that. Come to think of it, I know more about the sounds of owls than I do about humans. I don't know what sounds *people* make to find one another.

When Mother tells me about the swamp, she thinks she is sharing an act of bravery. She doesn't remember that my sisters and I were with the group of girls in the swamp that night, exposed, vulnerable, and terrified, or that to our little legs, crossing the stream was more like crossing a river.

Prickly Pear

The stems of the prickly pear are low and spreading, with flat pads that resemble a beaver's tail. The fruits of the cactus grow on the edges of the flat pads and are pear-shaped. They can range in color from green (less sweet) to a deep red (very sweet) and an array of orange shades in between. They are covered in little hairlike splinters called glochids. If they prick your skin, they can stick and be hard to find and surprisingly painful.

The entire cactus can be used for food. But protect yourself when picking the fruit. And before you eat it, you will need to remove the glochids, which you can burn off over an open flame. *Put the fruit on a stick, then slowly turn it over the flame, taking care not to set it on fire. As the glochids burn off, you may hear popping sounds or see little sparks fly off the fruit. Continue until all of the spots are blackened, indicating that the glochids are gone.*

Once you've removed the skin, you can eat the rest of the prickly pear fruit. It has small, hard seeds that you cannot bite through, but you can swallow. If that doesn't suit you, you can spit the seeds out as you chew on the fruit.

If you happen to get a few glochids in your fingers, arms, or legs while harvesting, they will be irritating, but they will eventually work themselves out of your skin.

I WANT TO BE LIKE AUNT BERNICE'S ROCKS, which she keeps in dozens of plastic trays in a little room attached to her garage.

Aunt Bernice's rocks aren't like Mormon rocks, large and looming; they are small and polished, colorful, rounded, soft to the touch. I want to be small and pretty like her rocks, which people want to touch and hold.

I keep my collection of the rocks Aunt Bernice has given me under my mattress next to the Sears catalog, so not even my sisters know I have them. Mother approves of rocks, of course, since they are part of God's creation, but she believes they belong outside, next to other wild things. If she knew about my collection, she would say I'm coveting or practicing idolatry or being vain and envisioning making them into jewelry, like a harlot, which maybe I am.

So I take out the rocks only at night, and I hold them like baby birds, stroking them surreptitiously, one by one, before putting them back in their nest.

I idolize the softness of these stones. I covet their comfort and worship their beauty. I'm not lovely, but I want to be surrounded by lovely things. I know this is a sin, wanting what I can't have. I'm rough and unruly, with knotty hair and piercing eyes, kind of like the prickly pear cactus we eat when we wander in the high desert, and not something anyone wants to touch or hold.

Mother believes in wedding rings, but she doesn't believe in other ornamentation. She won't let us get our ears pierced, because piercing your body makes you like Jezebel. When Mother was young, she pleased her father by making a vow to God that she would never defile her body by puncturing it in any way. So Mother doesn't have pierced ears, or tattoos. And she doesn't dye her hair either.

Once, when I asked her about this, she said if I ever do any of these things, I will be dead to her.

"I can only bend so far before I break," she says, "and I won't break for you. The Lord my God will keep me and protect me in the center of his will."

I can live without hair dye and tattoos, but I really, really want pierced ears. Of course, I don't tell Mother that. I keep my thoughts secret, like I keep many secrets, even the secrets of Aunt Bernice.

Bernice is Grandma's older sister, and Mother says she's a Quaker. She used to have a husband, but he died a couple of years ago, sometime after their fiftieth wedding anniversary, which Grandma let us celebrate with them at a family party before we moved to the Mountain. I had never been to a party and wanted to look like a real girl, so Grandma used a ripped sheet to make rag curls, threading my hair around each strip, winding them back up, and tying them off.

Our great-aunt Bernice is the only person I know who isn't part of the Field. My whole life, her home is the only home on the Outside we have been allowed to visit. When the Field has their leaders' dinner meetings, when one of the wives serves all the men (plus Grandma and Mother, because they are Grandpa's special counsel), there is tension at the Field, and no one wants us around. So Grandma drives us a few cities over to her sister's house. She drops us off, admonishing us to "be good."

In our family, visiting an Outsider's house is as close to blasphemy as we get. I've never even seen where Dad's mom, Grammie, lives, even though she's our blood relative.

When Grandma first took us to her sister's house, all we could see was trees. Aunt Bernice doesn't have grass or cement like other people do. She just has dirt and trees, which she doesn't clean up after, so leaves and branches and nuts litter her dirt driveway and make loud, crunchy noises when Grandma pulls in.

Aunt Bernice lets us collect avocados and pecans in brown paper sacks, enough to bring home and feed us all for a week. I used to think that's why we were allowed to go there, because we brought home food. That's an advantage, to be sure, but Aunt Bernice is also the only person who can stand having all of us kids over at the same time. And she doesn't make fun of us for the dresses we wear, which Mom makes out of pillowcases, using shoelaces as ties.

When Grandpa says being a Quaker is blasphemy and we aren't to visit, Grandma assures him her sister doesn't talk about religion with us. But I can assure you she does.

Maybe that's because I wore her down with my questions. Or maybe it's because I keep her secrets, like I keep her rocks.

But Aunt Bernice herself can't be kept from doing anything. Even Grandpa can't keep her from believing what she believes. He can't keep her from talking or laughing or praising Jesus with her big, wide voice and arms. She doesn't come to our church, not even to hear her sister play piano, maybe because she can't sit still, be quiet, or stay small.

Come to think of it, everything about Aunt Bernice is large.

When we pull into her driveway, Aunt Bernice hears the crunching and she comes out to greet us, wearing a long, flowing floral housedress, which looks like a tent. Grandma always wears a girdle, but Aunt Bernice doesn't even wear a bra or pantyhose or, usually, even shoes, so her body isn't contained the way other women's bodies are.

In fact, nothing about Aunt Bernice is contained.

Aunt Bernice lives on a suburban street, like other Southern California families, but she doesn't have a boundary between the front and the back of her land. Her house just sits plop-dab in the middle. And her house and yard are overflowing with every type of food you can imagine. It's not just the trees, which all produce something; it's also all her countertops and her cupboards and her shelves, which don't keep the cans of vegetables or boxes of cereal and rice and pasta and pancake mix from meandering all over the table and chairs.

If I ask her where to sit down in her house, she laughs and says, "Lord have mercy, move whatever you want to, child. You belong any place you want to be."

Aunt Bernice lets us do a lot of things no one else lets us do. Like eating anything we want, anytime we want, even if that includes cooking. She doesn't just let us use the toaster, like we do at Grandma's house; she also lets us use the stove and the oven and her various bowls and mixers. We can read whatever books she has in the house while we're there, play with her animals, watch her television, and stay up as long as we like.

On the Mountain, Dad restricts what we eat and weighs us every day to make sure we don't cheat. Everything is measured where we come from, but nothing is measured here. Nothing about Aunt Bernice's food or hugs or laughter has limits.

Becca and Danny are too young to understand the rules we break while we are there, but so far, Lizbeth and I seem to be in silent agreement not to tell. I think we learned this silence from Mother, who must know who her aunt is and how she lives but never mentions it, and, like many, things, hides it from Dad, who has never visited. Or maybe she just conveniently ignores what offends her, since God apparently doesn't hold her accountable for what she doesn't overtly know.

Of course, Lizbeth is a better girl than I am, and I don't think she would keep quiet about the blasphemy of Aunt

Bernice's religion. Aunt Bernice must know this too, because going to Quaker meetings is a secret we keep between us.

Aunt Bernice worships with her friends at meetings, which she says are a little like the churches we go to on the Trip, but they're not always on Sundays and you don't have to go in order to please God. She says God is pleased if you talk to him anywhere, any ol' day.

What happens in Aunt Bernice's friends' meetings isn't like what happens at our church, or any church I've ever visited. I ask her how she found these secret meetings, and she laughs her big belly laugh at me and says the friends have been around a long time, and she grew up in meetinghouses, and there's nothing secret about it. She says she and Grandma and their brother, Oscar, were all Quakers when they grew up in Kansas, because their parents raised them that way. In fact, Bernice and Oscar have been practicing this faith their whole lives, although she says, "We don't call ourselves Quakers. 'Quaker' is a word outside people use. On the inside, we just call ourselves Friends."

When Grandma met Grandpa, he told her being a Quaker was wrong, so she stopped going to meetings, but I don't think she really believes they're wrong. Grandma is proud of her family, because a long time ago they immigrated to Pennsylvania with William Penn.

I try to picture Grandma as a girl, loving her friends, but she is mostly loyal to Grandpa now and doesn't have friends, so I can't tell her about going to her sister's meetings. Aunt Bernice usually tells Lizbeth we are going out to get food and asks her to watch the other children, which Lizbeth never minds doing, because she is used to looking after the younger kids and because Aunt Bernice has a television and lets us watch it. Then she and I go to a meeting. And, of course, we bring home food.

At Aunt Bernice's friends' meetings, there is no one who stands up at the front like Grandpa does at our church, and there isn't a program they pass out with an order of service or any hymnals in the backs of the pews. They don't sing hymns or recite the doxology or the Lord's Prayer in unison. They don't sit on pews or even in rows, like all the other churches I've been to, where we go and sing and try to convince people there that they need to repent and prepare for the end times. We don't try to convince Quakers, because Grandpa says they don't listen to reason or listen to authority. They just sit in a circle and look at one another.

It makes me uncomfortable the way they look at one another in silence, and I want to bow my head and keep my eyes down, but if I do, I might miss what happens next. Not that much happens, most of the time. People just sit there, until one of the friends in the audience decides to share a story. When that person is done telling their story or just sharing an announcement or whatever, sometimes other people say "Praise the Lord" or "Amen," and sometimes someone will even sing a little piece of an old hymn, like it's rising up from within them.

When someone goes on too long, Aunt Bernice looks at me with sympathy and says, "Lord have mercy."

We haven't been to one of her meetings in a long time, but I like to remember how when we would get home from meetings, we would go to her workshop next to the garage and she would let me choose one of her polished rocks to take home with me. She whispered in my ear that I could make something pretty with them someday, something pretty like me.

No one except Aunt Bernice has ever told me I am pretty, but I think being pretty is why I will be performing in our annual circus this week.

The circus is the only place being pretty is allowed. In the circus, being pretty is more than allowed. At the circus, being pretty is celebrated.

I'm used to doing shows on the road, but in our road shows, we are witnessing and teaching people gently about God, and we make sure our costumes aren't flamboyant, so we don't lead the audience into temptation. When we witness before our road shows, we are respectful and careful not to let people know they'll be hearing about God when they get there. We march across the campgrounds playing instruments to tell people it's time to come to our show. They don't know we're a Bible band, because we play patriotic music, which makes them think we believe in our country. Which maybe we do, because even though he criticizes our government, Grandpa says our country was formed by godly people who came here to avoid religious persecution.

When we perform our plays and sing in churches all over the country, we travel in a caravan with vehicles carrying concessions and the sound and lighting systems, and a semitruck, which contains all the other elements of our set. When we are starting a new show, it often takes us five hours to put up our complicated set. The Field has members who can design and build and weld, and we set up ramps and rotating scenery. I am small and wiry, and I climb up the lighting trusses and put the bolts in. After a few weeks, we learn to put up the set in two hours and take it down in an hour. Unity and teamwork are key.

We start with a pre-show to warm up the audience. Since I was little, I've performed in the pre-shows as the conductor for Grandma's white poodle, Sois, which Grandma says is Spanish, not French. I step to the side with wide, grand gestures so the audience can see how special Sois is, playing the piano so elegantly with his paws. "Ladies and gentleman," I say dramatically, "I present to you . . . Sois!"

The audience applauds, and then we can tell them about God and ask them if they want to donate money. A lot of people donate money after they see Sois play the piano, even though they don't know God, but maybe someday they'll want to.

The holiness we hold ourselves accountable to on the inside sometimes contrasts with how we have to perform on the outside. It's like how Grandma always says music exists only to praise our Lord, and she knows all the hymns by heart and teaches them to us with reverence and precision. But she makes money for the family by teaching other people's children classical piano and bribing them with little white statuettes of composers like Brahms and Beethoven, Schumann, Mozart, Wagner, Verdi, and Chopin, who aren't apostles or maybe even believers. This might look like idolatry from the outside, but Grandma does it because Grandpa needs the money for his boys.

Some of the boys who follow Grandpa aren't really boys anymore. They grow old following him and turn into disciples, and one of these disciples is Houdini II. He does all the same things the real Houdini did, but that Houdini died, so that makes our Houdini special, like he was raised from the dead. Sometimes our Houdini submerges himself underwater in a straitjacket and has to get out of it before he drowns.

Houdini II's theatrics are more popular than our proselytizing, so Grandpa uses him in the circus to make money. Since I've become popular as a poodle conductor, sometimes I get to be Houdini's assistant.

Maybe I'm just good at selling illusions, because I've been doing it in one form or another since I was a small child. Before we moved to the Mountain, I spent countless days of my childhood on street corners in big cities, outside of banks, or going door-to-door, selling circus tickets or candy. If I was asked to leave, I would politely smile and appear to acquiesce, and then find another house, or another street corner, or get into the elevator and go down to the next floor and keep asking. I was taught to avoid the authorities, to never tell anyone my real name or where I came from, and to put the money I received in a specific envelope I hid in my shirt. No matter what strangers told me, I was never to touch the money. Even if they told me to buy food or water with it, I was forbidden to touch the money, and I never did.

We are taught that everything Outsiders tell us is a lie. So I've spent years skirting all questions, refusing the hospitality of strangers, finding strange ways to feed my hunger.

Sometimes when I'm waiting to get picked up, I take off my shoes and slide my holey socks over my hands so I can peel the skin off the prickly pear cacti that grow in the succulent garden in the Bank of America parking lot.

"Be good," Grandma tells me, so I am quiet as I take people's money and give it to the Field.

There was a routine and a script. We would stand in the bushes in front of a bank and jump out in front of people, loudly chanting, often startling them:

"Hey out there, here's your chance,
Jump for joy, sing and dance.
No one before in the history of man
Could match this offer, and no one can.
It's the greatest opportunity.
If you miss it now, don't cry to me.
So step right up, be first in line,
Just sign your name on this dotted line."

Sometimes I would sell with a partner, but usually, I worked alone. I was one of the higher producers, so I often worked twelve-hour shifts, six days a week, and I handed over every penny I received to the Field.

Everything we sell helps, but the circus is our biggest moneymaker; the operating budget of the Field is largely sustained by its success. We sell about fifty thousand tickets, although only a fraction of those people who buy tickets actually come to a show. We have space for about fifteen hundred people at each showing, but some people come more than one day. When they get there, we sell them food, and game tickets, and trinkets.

The circus is how God provides, so that we can be ready for when Jesus will come back *as a thief in the night* and end the world as we know it, and we can all run to the mountains and survive Armageddon. Because we know that *in the last days it shall come to pass, that the mountain of the house of the Lord shall be established in the top of the mountains, and it shall be exalted above the hills; and people shall flow unto it.*

The Field is good at creating fear. But here's the thing about circuses that they don't tell you: They're like magic. They work only if people want to believe.

At the circus, we have elephants and trapeze artists, and Houdini II hangs upside down from a helicopter in a strait-jacket on a burning rope, and he tries to get out of the strait-jacket so he can climb up to the helicopter and not fall on his head into the people in the audience, who look up in fear of that very thing.

The Houdini act I'll be in during this circus is one I've performed a lot on the road. This act involves a black box with lots of holes about a quarter inch in diameter across all sides. Houdini calls up two volunteers from the audience to check out the box. The volunteers pick up the box, open and close the lid, and verify that it is solid. Then Houdini puts someone inside the box. Sometimes that person is me.

Houdini II transports the audience to a world where anything is possible, everything feels real, and the unbelievable becomes believable. It's not about the illusions or the applause or any real sleight of hand. It's about his ability to make the audience believe in him.

It works best when the magician believes the story he is telling to the audience. And it doesn't hurt if the assistant does too, and so I make myself believe what we're doing is magic.

Houdini II waves his arms and inserts steel rods into the box, in one side and out the other, crisscrossing in the middle. The audience gasps. Certainly, he is spearing the little girl inside, but no one hears the girl cry out, so no one comes up to save her and Houdini continues to insert more steel rods.

A real magician never tells the truth of his magic, but I'm not a magician. I'm not the man manipulating the steel rods. I'm just the girl who gets speared, so I can say whatever I want.

Here's the secret: There is no magic in Houdini's box. I maneuver around the steel rods by being flexible. It's hard to breathe in there, especially when Houdini takes a long time to insert the rods for dramatic effect, but I can contort myself to fit around them and I can hold my breath for a very long time.

When the box is sufficiently pierced with overlapping rods, Houdini pauses and the audience sits in silence, like they do at the Quaker meetings. Then as Houdini pulls out each rod, one by one, a trickle of air wafts through the box, and I begin to breathe again.

When he finishes taking out all the rods, the audience sees a black box that looks like it's riddled with bullet holes. Houdini II opens the lid carefully, and the audience anticipates the carnage. Then I stand up and smile, waving my hands and showing the audience: I have survived.

Nettles

Nettles are a perennial herb with stout, unbranched stems and tiny green flowers that hang loosely in clusters at the base of the leaves. They are known for their vicious stinging properties, but they are also a nutritious edible plant that tastes mildly like spinach.

Stems are upright and rigid and the leaves are heart-shaped, fine-toothed, and tapered at the ends. The entire plant is covered with little, stiff hairs, mostly on the underside of the leaves and stems, which release formic acid when touched.

For hundreds of years, people have recorded using nettles to treat painful muscles and joints, eczema, arthritis, gout,

*and anemia. The leaves are rich in calcium and iron and you
can eat them steamed or boiled.*

*Nettles are common in damp places below 9,000 feet ele-
vation. If you don't have gloves, you can still harvest them.
The hairs on nettles grow angling down the stem, so if you
grab from the top, with your fingers pushing the hairs in the
direction they grow, you can usually avoid getting stung.*

DAD BELIEVES SHOES SHOULD BE WORN at all times, even
indoors. He says this is a proper way to conduct oneself and
a sensible way to prevent injury.

Dad says he believes in being sensible. But injuries aren't
something we avoid.

When we don't respond quickly enough when Dad wants
something, he doesn't yell. Sometimes he hits, but usually he
calmly glares and slowly says, "If you don't clean up this
flophouse, I'll squish you like a stinkbug."

Since we've come to the Mountain, Dad has been teaching us something he calls comfort control, which means we
practice putting ourselves in a wide range of uncomfortable
environments and learn to adapt to the discomfort. Maybe
he has been doing this since we were toddlers, but it's not
until we moved to the Mountain that he had a proper canvas
for this project. Or maybe I'm just now old enough to be
cognizant of the difference between trusting him and trusting myself.

Everyone at the Field trusts men more than women. They
say they're trusting God, but only men tell us what God's

word means, so it feels like maybe that's who we're really trusting. It seems unfair to me that all three parts of God are male, but Mother says you can't trust a woman, because of Eve, who ate of the tree of knowledge, because she couldn't leave well enough alone.

Dad teaches us not to trust our body or its signals. We learn to override our body's warnings, convincing ourselves that comfort and care are sin. We collect rocks in the desert like it's penance. We don't bring water, not because Dad wants us to learn to find it within the plants, but because he wants us to suffer the pains of thirst and be humbled, to know only the Lord our God can save us. We hike in the snow in tennis shoes, and we keep our wet socks on after and practice not complaining. We get blisters on our hands from chopping and carrying logs, but even when they bleed, we don't use gloves, bandages, or aspirin.

Dad teaches us to adhere to the US Army's principles of loyalty, duty, respect, selfless service, honor, integrity, and personal courage. We reenact drills straight out of his army basic training, except we use BBs instead of real bullets in our guns. Mom won't let us use real guns, although I know where Dad hides his.

Dad was drafted to serve in the Korean War, and he spent short stints stationed in Fort Ord and Fort Irwin while he waited to be shipped overseas. After two years, he was never shipped anywhere and never saw combat, so he spent a lot of time training, a lot of time thinking, and a lot of time learning the army's belief system, which he has embraced as a proper mindset for serving in the army of God.

Our life on earth is a source of perpetual tension, he reminds us. This is the devil's domain, he says, and the earth is something to overcome. God ordained us to assert our dominion over the fish and the fowl, over all the beasts of burden that walk the earth. This includes, of course, our primal selves, long ago cast out of Eden.

We are at constant war against our flesh, resisting cold or heat or fatigue through the power of our minds, overcoming the desire for affection, comfort, and security.

Living in the mess hall, we already know how to do KP and police call, which Dad learned during his military days, and we wake up before sunrise to timed trail runs and jumping rope for a minute without missing. If we miss, we start again. We have white-glove tests, and we hike in the snow and rain with loaded backpacks. We swim in Jackson Lake with clothes and shoes on, at the command of a whistle. He throws things at us randomly, and we catch whatever is thrown at us, softening into the thrust, like a punch.

Preparing for war is an essential component of growing up. As the army taught him, Dad teaches us:

I will always place the mission first.
I will never accept defeat.
I will never quit.
I will never leave a fallen comrade.

We build an outdoor chapel where the Field family can worship. When the boys come up, we showcase a mannequin, onto which we dress layers of military garb. We *put*

*on the whole armour of God, that we may be able to stand
against the wiles of the devil.*

And we sing while we ceremoniously place *the helmet of
salvation* on the wooden head, *the breastplate of righteous-
ness* on the planked trunk, *the sword of the Spirit* into the
rigid fingers of one hand, *the shield of faith* in the other, *to
quench the fiery darts of the wicked.*

When the boys are up here, I sing with them at chapel,
because I've sung in churches all across the United States and
Canada and Mexico on the Trip, and I'm a strong soprano.
"*Christ, the royal Master, leads against the foe. Forward into
battle, see his banner go.*" We sing in unison at first, and then
break off into a four-part harmony when Grandpa gives the
signal.

Today I have a solo. My thin, high, clear voice extends
into the mountain air: "*Onward then, ye people, join our
happy throng. Blend with ours your voices in the triumph
song.*"

This isn't a happy throng, though. This is a war of prin-
cipalities, and we march as if to war, *with the cross of Jesus
going on before.*

When Dad trains us in his army ways, we don't wrestle
against flesh and blood, but against the rulers of the darkness
of the world, against spiritual wickedness in high places. We
gird ourselves with Truth.

We are told the best way to withstand the temptations of
the flesh, with which Outsiders will try to defile our bodies, is
to teach ourselves not to desire anything by repudiating pleasure in all forms. This includes tobacco, liquor, tasty foods,

worldly music, entertainment for entertainment's sake, reading (other than the Bible), and anything that inspires laughter or affection. We aren't even allowed to hug one another.

One of our Dad's favorite stories is how his army superiors would order the grunts to move all the rocks from one side of the building to the other. When they had finished, their superiors ordered them to move all the rocks back to where they started.

Our father doesn't tell us whether the point of this activity is to obey without question, to see suffering and perseverance as war preparations, or to learn to accept the sheer idiocy of leadership. He just says doing what you're told to do builds character. Even when it doesn't make sense.

We move a lot of rocks.

Sometimes while Dad is going through his daily rituals of weighing us or making us jump rope, I ask him questions, which he's better at answering than Mother is.

"Did you have to shoot anyone to protect our country?"

"As a mechanic in the army, the Lord was with me, protecting and guiding me so I could keep things running for the Field when I got out. The Lord gave me opportunities to play sports and teach his word to the soldiers."

Dad spent a lot of time playing sports in the army. He played baseball and fast-pitch softball and basketball, his favorite. But I already know enough about sports. I ask him if he saw anyone get killed.

"God protected me and used me as a beacon to teach other young men. I spent my first year at Fort Ord playing a little volleyball and basketball at company level. My second year, I spent at Fort Irwin, where we played basketball against other bases. We had fifty-three wins and four losses. And I got to catch for a professional baseball pitcher who played for the Washington Senators."

There's something Dad's not telling me. There's no way his army training made him who he is. Lots of kids at the Field have dads who were drafted, but none of them do training rituals like we do and none of them talk about flophouses or stinkbugs. I think his story comes from somewhere darker than his military days.

And I'm committed to finding out.

On some level, Dad must have needed what the army gave him, because he quotes its tenets more than he quotes the Bible. I ask a lot of questions about his past, and he's vague in his responses, but I add his answers to what Mother and Grandpa say when he's not in the room, and I've pieced together some of his story.

Dad is an only child, and he didn't really have a father after he was seven, because that's when his dad was drafted and deployed to Italy, where he served for two years during World War II. Unlike my dad, his father saw people die and he came back angry and sad.

When Dad was twelve, his mother executed a stealthy getaway for the two of them. They rode on a bus across country to forge a new home in California. She didn't tell him they were leaving.

Dad didn't know where they were going on that bus, and he didn't get to say goodbye to anyone, not on the day they left, or ever. He never spoke to his father again, not even on the phone, and when his father died four years later, he didn't find out. Eventually, he learned that his father had died of pneumonia in a motel room in Southern California, a man alone in his early forties, a mile from his estranged wife and teenage son. Dad didn't know his father had arrived here or that he'd died here until recently, when he visited his military grave in San Diego.

When Dad and Grammie arrived in California, he started playing sports after school at the Field, an organization for boys that my mother's father ran. Mother remembers meeting him when she was eight and he was thirteen. He was dropping off a Christmas gift for her father, and she thought he was the most handsome boy she had ever seen.

Even now, she says he is the only boy she has ever held hands with or kissed. Both of our parents waited until the altar at their wedding to touch, because Mother is good at doing what's right and Dad does what her father taught him to. She says she would never disappoint her father, and neither would our Dad.

I picture Grandpa standing behind the altar, while my future husband and I huddle on the church's kneelers and bow our bodies, while Grandpa raises his hands, approving of our union, just like he's doing in the pictures of him officiating Mother and Dad's wedding.

Mother makes all her children vow to wait for our first kiss until the altar and we promise, even writing down our commitment, so she can see we mean it. When I turned nine, I picked a swath of nettles, tore up my missive, and put the little paper shreds, along with the nettles, into a mug of boiling water. Then I drank down the words like tea, so my body would remember.

I didn't yet know how to manipulate the stinging hairs on nettles, so my hands burned for the next three days.

Grandpa spends most of his time with the young men who started their training when they were children, forsaking their families to follow him. Mostly from broken homes, these boys feel honored to have such a significant place in his world. They believe God called them to be devoted to Grandpa and that, through his work, they will bring light to the world. Some of them play a special role as a personal assistant to him in some way, helping him with his clothing and ties, or giving him massages in one of the campers.

Dad was one of Grandpa's earliest disciples, and he believes Grandpa knows the will of God in all things, that even his temper mirrors Yahweh's.

They say that back in the day, Grandpa was tall, handsome, intelligent, full of passion and charm, charismatic enough to inspire people to give up their freedom and devote their lives to him and the jealous God he serves.

Our lives are at the mercy of his whims.

I've been listening to Grandpa's devotional talks for years, and I know I'm still a sinner, because inside I don't worship him like everyone else does. He doesn't hug or kiss me or tell me I'm special, but I think that's because we're all special at the Field; we are God's chosen people.

As descendants by blood, I think the only real distinction my cousins and I have from other leaders' kids is knowing Grandpa would kill us if God asks him to.

I am glad we live on the Mountain so I will have some-where to hide when Grandpa gets the instruction to use his knife to sacrifice us for the kingdom.

Grandpa is clear that the Bible is the literal word of God and that Abraham was righteous in his attempt to kill Isaac, and Mother also says it's important not to get too attached, because God requires us to sacrifice our children for the greater good.

As the oldest grandchildren, Lizbeth, Becca, and I are kept near Grandpa, because he can't trust Mother to train us up in the way we should go. Or at least, this is what used to happen before we came to the Mountain. While we don't see him as much now, we are each required to go with him as his companion for ten weeks on the Trip with the boys. The summer I was eight, it was my turn.

So I went on the Trip with Grandpa, my dad, and seventy boys, across the country for ten weeks, performing in a play called *Penniless*.

We all live together when we are on the Trip, so we develop a common language we can use to protect ourselves when we feel threatened by the world's values.

Enter ye in at the strait gate: for wide is the gate, and broad is the way, that leadeth to destruction, and many there be which go in thereat: Because strait is the gate, and narrow is the way, which leadeth unto life, and few there be that find it.

Mother wasn't with us on the Trip when I was eight, but I was held tight behind the gate of Grandpa's rules. She believed in *God, the Father Almighty, creator of heaven and earth, and in Jesus Christ his only son, our Lord, who was conceived by the Holy Spirit, born of the Virgin Mary, and ordered by his own father to suffer under Pontius Pilate, was crucified, died, and buried.* She, too, believed that, like Abraham, she was called to sacrifice her children as a testament to her devotion to our Lord. In exchange, God would bless her, and multiply her seed *as the stars of the heaven, and as the sand which is upon the sea shore.*

Mother considered her children lilies of the field, trusting that God would provide in his own way and time. So, of course, she let me go.

I LISTEN TO GRANDPA, but I don't know how all the stories I hear fit. Grandpa gives me a new King James Bible for my birthday, and I memorize passages from it and from *Foxe's Book of Martyrs*, which was published in 1563 and gives detailed descriptions of the persecutions of Christians, including graphic depictions of torture and enduring suffering until death.

I don't know if it's better to be in armies and kill people or to be a martyr and get tortured for being a Christian. So I decide to read the whole Bible cover to cover and see for myself what is true. I don't think my family will like this, because they cite certain parts and leave out others. But I vow to God to finish every word of the King James Bible before I turn nine.

I do this in secret in the back of the Winnebago while Grandpa snores and the string of the pulley to the cabinet door swishes back and forth like a pendulum. I gaze hypnotically, and I pray rhythmically, softly, a prayer as a mantra I have come to believe will elicit a miracle:

"Our Father who art in heaven, Lord God above, ruler of all things, please give me a sign. If you are listening to me, if my life is of any significance to you, if you have a plan, please stop swinging. Make the tassel stop. Make it stand still, like the Red Sea, with the walls of water still, like unsung statues, like the sun, how you made it stand still in the sky until the nation of Israel defeated its enemies. Since you can make still the water and stop the sun, and you can bring your son back from the dead, make this little string stop. Show me you are listening. Show me you know what is happening down here. Please still the tassel."

In the evenings, I kneel next to a prop bed in a little white nightgown and sing to audiences in KOA campgrounds across the country. "*Now I lay me down to sleep . . . I pray the Lord my soul to keep . . . If I should die before I wake . . . I pray the Lord my soul to take.*"

And then later each night, I read with a penlight, cross-referencing like Mother does when she is learning the scientific terms for all the flora and fauna, marking up passages I feel are contradictions, as if constructing a map for a prison escape.

Every day in the Winnebago, as we traverse the southern states, performing circus acts as a pre-show before the proselytizing plays, I pray for the tassel to stand still.

It may be that the Lord wants to test my patience, like he did Job's. Maybe I'm not in tune with his words. Maybe that's the problem. I'm not a precious stone or a precious metal because I haven't been tested. I think of what I know of Jehovah, what my grandfather has personified for me, as he sits like a refiner and purifier of silver, burning away the dross.

So I pray:

"Dear God, I will show my allegiance to you and read your book, every word of your book, starting now. I will read your Holy Book cover to cover.

"In the beginning there was the Word, and the Word was with God, and the Word was God. . . . And the Word was made flesh.

"You are the word. I am the flesh. Let your word become my flesh. Let my flesh become your word. I begin at the beginning, when God created the heavens and the earth."

There is plenty of time to read, because I'm not allowed to play with the boys or sit with them at evening meals. Grandpa says boys are different, that unlike girls, they have physical needs. So I spend many hours in many campgrounds in many states, watching groups of boys running away to wherever boys go.

But for two hours each afternoon, Grandpa holds daily prayer meetings in the Winnebago with his closest, most loyal disciples. My uncles don't have to be in there, because they already know Grandpa and God, and someone has to watch the other boys as they run around doing whatever boys do.

I wait outside and hold private devotions while Grandpa and his disciples commune with God in the Winnebago.

On one sunny afternoon, one of my uncles speaks to me. "I'm taking these guys over to the river. You want to come along?"

My eyes wander to the small group of gangly adolescents restlessly flicking one another with towels. "I don't know if I can. Do you think he would approve?" I nod toward the camper, where I'm sure Grandpa, omniscient and omnipotent, like God or Santa Claus, pulls back the curtain regularly to watch me.

"I don't know," my uncle says, "but how about if we don't ask? I'll get you back before they're done."

I stare at the curtains on the windows of the Winnebago, but they don't seem to be moving. I'm sure I will get in trouble if I follow my uncle, but I am tired of sitting and tired of the bugs and tired of being good.

Lizbeth wouldn't disappoint Grandpa. But I will.

The first day, I watch the boys from the sidelines, listening to their roars of pain and pleasure, as they jump in the lake.

Grandpa doesn't say anything when his prayer meeting lets out, so the next day, in another campground, I follow my uncle again.

I still ride and sleep and eat in the Winnebago with Grandpa, but I live for my uncle's afternoon calls. As we travel up into the central northern states and through the lower Canadian provinces, water is everywhere. Cold, icy, daring water, which makes the boys whoop.

Eventually, I learn to jump from overhanging rocks into the moving water below. I learn to dog-paddle against the current until I can find a rock to grab hold of. I catch my breath and look for something else to hang on to. When the water is particularly rough, an uncle sends one of the older boys to guide me.

One day, I jump off a rock into a current and get pulled under. I can't breathe, and I can't swim strongly enough to find my way out of the current, back to the boys. I can't even keep my head above water. I stop flailing and become still, practicing what I learned on the Mountain.

Pay attention to what's around you. Don't panic. Look for the gift, because it is always there. Survive fear. Survive with faith.

I become soft in the water, letting it hold me, flowing where it wants to take me. Mother taught us that water is the earth's blood, that it gives life to all beings, like a womb. We must honor it in all its forms, from the blood in our veins to the sap in the trees, to the undulations of rivers and streams.

Don't be afraid. Be competent.

I see a fallen log and reach out for a branch, pulling myself into the dead tree, clinging to it until I can breathe again. Then I climb out onto the bank and whistle my best owl sound, a signal to my uncle, so he can find me.

Even though my hair and my clothes are wet, Grandpa never asks me where I've been, and I never bring up my afternoon excursions. My uncle is mindful to get me back before the meetings are out, so I am sitting at an appropriate spot when the men descend from the camper. I look up at their holy faces and wonder if perhaps Grandpa hasn't been pulling aside the curtains to check up on me after all.

But in the end, after all the waters I have arisen from like a baptism, after reading all of the words in the Bible, God does not have mercy upon me. God does not make that tassel stand still. We drive through Virginia and Maryland, New York and Pennsylvania and Ohio, through Wisconsin and Minnesota, into the Dakotas, and I sing in my high, sweet voice, night after night, and conduct Sois on the piano to laughter and applause, and the tassel swings side to side, obeying the laws of physics.

Elderberry

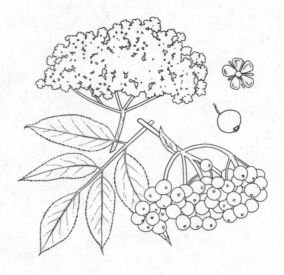

The elderberry is a deciduous shrub with compound, oppo-site leaves two to four inches long and numerous cream-col-ored sweet-smelling flowers. It blooms from March through September.

You can eat its flowers and ripe berries raw, but—take care!—the leaves, stems, and unripe berries are toxic, so make sure to pick and eat only ripe blue or black berries. (Red berries are also poisonous.) If the flowers and berries upset your stomach, try boiling them.

Elderberries are a highly desirable source of food for humans and for many songbirds, so you may be able to enjoy the sound of music while you are harvesting.

OUR DIRT ROAD IS LINED WITH MILKWEED, which Mother says doesn't belong here. She says those nasty flowers are a pernicious weed, and poisonous, to boot, and we should never eat them, no matter how hungry we are.

I like the word *pernicious*. I write it down.

I have almost finished the Bible, and every time I see a word I don't know, I write it down in the Sears catalog. I write the words and pronounce them out loud the best I can. And then I look them up in Mother's concordance when she's not around, so that I can see all the places the Bible uses these words and start to make sense of them. I have been working my way through the words on my list: *Betrothed. Zeal. Exhort. Leviathan. Tribulation. Omnipotent. Pestilence. Laud.*

I don't know things other American children know, like the names of presidents, the years of wars, or the capitals of countries or states, but I know a lot of words.

The Lord will come back *as a thief in the night,* so I have to be prepared. I'm nine now, and I'm responsible for my own soul, so I go back and reread Nehemiah and Lamentations, Obadiah and Habakkuk and Zephaniah, and I keep reading forward through the New Testament too. And then I go back and forth between them, comparing books written by the prophets to the letters sent to the churches, called epistles, and I reread the Psalms while I'm reading the crowning glory of Revelation, which almost chokes me with its numbers and symbols. I draw diagrams to help me imbibe the vitriol of the whore of Babylon and to quell my fear of the beast and the four horsemen of the Apocalypse.

Every time I read a passage that seems to contradict something I read in an earlier book of the Bible, I put that in a column. I fill the catalog with my questions.

Dad has been away on the Trip for months, and Mother's rhythms are different when he's not around. We don't eat meals together or have a bedtime. There are no timed jump-roping sessions or runs or weigh-ins or commands for lights-out. We move to the tempo of our curiosities, sidelined only by hunger or fatigue, feeding ourselves or sleeping when we run out of steam.

During the days, I hike around the Mountain, eating elderberries and thinking about what I have read. I speak to myself in the language and cadence of the King James Bible, having conversations in my head with the word of God. My thoughts are organized by archaic translations of writings that are thousands of years old, but this feels like food to me. After all, *a man's belly shall be satisfied with the fruit of his mouth; and with the increase of his lips shall he be filled.*

And I fill myself with words.

I have read through every *he begat* in the Old Testament, which is the lineage of Jesus Christ, and I note there are exactly four women included: Tamar, Rahab, Ruth, and Bathsheba. I try to figure out why these specific women are named in the lineage, why others like Sarah and Rachel, who are also ancestors of Jesus, aren't named, and what role these women played in the world of men, which is the only world I know and likely the only world they knew too.

I shouldn't be thinking about this, because Grandpa doesn't talk about girls except as temptresses, but I keep going

back to these girls who are named, and even though I continue reading chronologically, I also go back to my marked
passages.

I have been taught not to question, but I use a highlighter
I pilfered from Mother's supply drawer to draw attention
to what interests me. I can't ask God, but I highlight the
words of Ruth and Rahab, and I carefully read what is said
about Tamar and Bathsheba, who don't even speak in their
own story. These girls don't follow rules the way I've been
taught girls should, but here they are listed in the Bible as
great-grandmothers of Jesus.

Tamar seems like an exception to every rule I've been
taught about what it means to be a good girl. I mean, Judah
was supposedly a godly man, and he chose Tamar to be the
wife of his wicked oldest son. When that son died, he asked
his next son, Onan, to have a baby with Tamar in the name
of his brother, but Onan would just lie with Tamar and spill
his seed on the ground instead of getting her pregnant. Tamar
was at her wits' end, because she was nothing without a husband or a baby, so she disguised herself and pretended to be
a prostitute to trick Judah into giving her a baby. And he did!
He impregnated her while he thought she was a prostitute.
If she hadn't kept his staff as payment, she would have been
stoned to death for having a child out of wedlock, but she
was able to prove to Judah that it was his child. So, she got to
keep the baby and pretend her first husband was the father.
And her son became a direct ancestor of Jesus. Why?

I want to talk to someone about girls in the Bible, and
what role they play in a world of men, but Mother isn't the

right one to ask. She has patience for strangers' questions, but she gets frustrated with mine.

Sometimes I sneak around like Rahab's spies, listening to Mother when she teaches people out on the trails. She hates when I listen in on her, but I do it anyway, because I miss our training trips and I want to learn what she knows.

Mother is president of the San Gabriel Mountains Interpretive Association, and she spends more time with Ranger Harold and the resident entomologist, Jarvis, than she does with us. But she has learned a lot about insects from Jarvis, so now we know which ones to eat. And she says her work there will help us during the coming Apocalypse.

The Big Pines Ranger Station is the only public place I know close enough to walk to from our house, but we aren't allowed to. Mother says it's important to let Ranger Harold and Jarvis do their work, which doesn't include supervising children.

I've never thought of myself as a child, and it's been years since anyone has supervised any of us, so I suspect there is more to that story.

I'm holding on to the pieces of many stories, and eventually, I'll piece them all together.

I like to listen to Mother teach people things they don't know, and I write down the words I learn on the inside of my wrist to put in my catalog later. That's how I know milkweed isn't as pernicious as she told us it is.

When she takes visitors on hikes, she points out plants and tells them what they are and why they should care. "This common milkweed has spread all over this mountain from people who brought it here for residential use," she'd say. "It doesn't belong here, but it gives us a healthy butterfly population, so no one removes it."

The visitors nod and say nice things about butterflies as Mother continues, giving them more information than they want to know. "There are one hundred fifteen species of milkweed, and most animals avoid contact with all of them, because of the cardiac glycoside compounds, which are harmful to most mammals. But four hundred fifty insects, including flies, bees, and wasps, can safely feed on milkweed. Monarch butterflies take particular advantage of this poison and use it as a defense. During the larval stage, they attach to milkweed, extracting and storing the toxin. They store milkweed in their tissues, rendering them toxic to other animals, and birds find them distasteful, so they leave them alone. If you want to encourage butterflies in your area, grow milkweed in your gardens."

"So anything that tries to eat these butterflies will die?" a visitor asks.

"Well, it's mostly an olfactory illusion," Mother explains. "Monarchs accumulate relatively little of the toxic compounds, and they are likely edible. But because of the smell, the birds don't know that and the butterflies flourish."

I spy on Mother during the day and then stay up late into the night studying the words in the Bible because I can't sleep anyway. I am afraid of falling into the earth, of being swallowed up when the big one hits. Reading and learning the words in the Bible is how I will recognize the signs of the beast and know how to flee.

I have been out for hours this morning, and I am barefoot, since I have used my socks as a container for several fistfuls of elderberries. I have acclimated to eating elderberries raw, but today I have collected enough to boil them into a jelly, and I am excited to make use of my harvest.

As I walk barefoot down the Mountain toward our house, I hear music. Either I am imagining this or the angels have come, like strangers to Sodom, and have filled our mountain with their songs. I am scared to go in the house, but I am even more scared to stay out. If the angel of the Lord is upon us, I want to see him. I want to know what I'm up against.

I open the door quietly and see the back of someone across the room on a bench, playing Mozart's Piano Sonata no. 16 in C Major. I didn't even know we had a piano. I stand and stare.

It doesn't look like an angel. It looks like my mother.

Grandma used to play all of Mozart's sonatas, and the sounds feel comforting. I close my eyes and listen to the music, waiting until she has finished the song before I walk closer.

When she turns around, she abruptly closes the lid over the keyboard.

"I didn't know you knew how to play the piano," I say.

"I don't," she answers, walking toward the kitchen.

"But I just heard you playing."

"No, you didn't," she says.

"I heard you."

She is pouring herself some coffee and doesn't answer, so I try a different tactic, "When did we get a piano?"

"George's family had it delivered today."

"I thought we were George's family," I say.

George is one of the men from the Field who has been living with us this past year, one of Grandpa's boys, who belongs to us now. When you commit your life to the Field, you give up whatever life and family and belongings you had before. Sometimes Grandpa sends wayward men up to the Mountain to work on the land by the sweat of their brow and become righteous before they are allowed to work with boys at the Field.

She doesn't respond, so I follow her to her room and try again, "Where is George's real family, and why would they give us a piano?"

"We're his real family now. Maybe he'll play for you someday," she offers. Then she closes her door to me, but I can still hear her talking on the other side. "Lord knows, I can't play the piano. Never could. Your grandma said all I could ever do was make noise."

Mother says eavesdropping is a sin, but it doesn't say so in the Bible. I mean, Esther eavesdropped. How else would she have known about Haman's plot against the Jews? Isn't it prudent to know the thoughts of your enemies?

There is a black rotary phone sitting on a wood desk in the corner of my parents' bedroom, with the manual typewriter Mother pounds away on long into the nights, now that we have a house. We aren't allowed to make phone calls, not even to our relatives at the Field, because phone calls are expensive and God doesn't provide for people who waste.

Our phone is connected through a party line, which means the line is shared with all the other camps across the mountain. Sometimes when the house is empty, I softly pick up the phone and cradle the handle, checking to see if I can hear anyone talking on the other end. If I can, I wrap the mouthpiece with a washcloth and listen in.

And he said unto them, Is a candle brought to be put under a bushel, or under a bed? and not to be set on a candlestick? For there is nothing hid, which shall not be manifested; neither was any thing kept secret, but that it should come abroad. If any man have ears to hear, let him hear. And he said unto them, Take heed what ye hear: with what measure ye mete, it shall be measured to you: and unto you that hear shall more be given. For he that hath, to him shall be given: and he that hath not, from him shall be taken even that which he hath.

I've asked Mother who all these people are on our party line, and she says the only one she knows is Ranger Harold, whom I still haven't met. She says the rest of the families at the other camps are not our people, so I'm not to talk to them. I never *talk*, so maybe I'm not disobeying her when I listen to their voices. Rahab knows you can learn a lot from listening to other people's conversations.

A man from one of the other camps once told his brother on the phone that California is overdue for a historic earthquake. He said the most recent large quake on the San Andreas Fault was in 1857; before that, there was one in 1812. I do the math. There were forty-five years between those earthquakes, and it's been 120 years since the last big one.

I'm not right with God, and he might use the earthquake to elicit the Second Coming, in which case, I will not be spared. I'm not good like Lizbeth, so I will either be gobbled up by the earth, descending into hell, where there is weeping and gnashing of teeth, or I'll be buried alive.

Grandpa tells a lot of stories about people being buried alive and other evil things Outsiders do to one another. He tells a lot of stories of evil men, some of whom murder young women and chop up their bodies and mail the various body parts to people who loved them. He tells us that's why we're not allowed to use public bathrooms, even when we're out selling things.

I'm more afraid of falling into the earth and being swallowed up when the big one hits than I am getting chopped up by a man hiding in a bathroom. At least with a man, I might have the chance to fight back.

The Word was with God . . . and the Word was made flesh. You are the word. I am the flesh. Let your word become my flesh. Let my flesh become your word.

I'VE SLEPT AT THE HOUSES of everyone at the Field, and I have gotten good at listening in on what adults say when they think the children are asleep. I can tell you what scares them, how they pray, and whether they whisper or yell when they're angry.

I think a lot about the difference between the way the other families live at the Field and the way we live here on the Mountain.

We used to be close to the Mitchells and the Washingtons, who each have a daughter exactly my age. All six of our parents have grown up together under the purview of Grandpa since they were teenagers, but it doesn't seem like Mother talks to either Mrs. Washington or Mrs. Mitchell anymore.

I want to know why, but I know Mother won't tell me her feelings or any personal details about anyone at the Field. Instead, I ask Mother about the Second Coming, and whether everyone at the Field will rise to heaven except us. Will we be the only ones who stay back and turn people to Christ during the millennium of darkness? How come the Mitchells and the Washingtons don't have to learn survival skills?

"Are we the only ones who will need to survive and lead the army of God?" I ask her. "Who will be in the army we're leading?"

"Grandpa sent us up here to prepare for the end of times. Your job is to be righteous, to resist the temptations of the world and to learn to survive. God will take care of the rest."

Mother is cleaning her traps and cages and is more receptive than usual, so I keep going. "At the end of the thousand years," I ask, "will all the animals be extinct, like the dinosaurs? Or can some of them live in the darkness?"

"The earth will go back to how it was before we came," she explains, "and then we will get to go up and live in heaven, with any animals God chooses."

"So when God parted the face of the deep, and the world was without form and void, were the dinosaurs living in all that darkness?"

"Of course not," she replied. "All living things need light."

"So there were dinosaurs in the Garden of Eden?"

She doesn't answer, but I stay quiet while she feeds a mouse to a California king snake. She moves on to feeding the kangaroo rats, and I think she is done with me, but then she continues. "No, they were outside of the garden, but after Eve disobeyed God, humans had to survive with them in the antediluvian period, until they all drowned in the flood."

"Why didn't Noah take a pair of each of them into the ark with him, like he did all the other animals?"

"So humans could flourish."

"But what about the fossils? They're older than the Bible."

"God has all sorts of ways to test our faith. Don't believe everything they tell you. Trusting science is like Eve eating from the tree of knowledge, and look where that got us."

I think she is leaving something out, but I love the word *antediluvian*. I repeat it over and over to myself. When I am grown up, I want to know all the words.

I go back to Genesis, looking for something that might allude to dinosaurs. I read through the books of law, and Judges, and the Chronicles to see how they influence the prophets, and Psalms and Proverbs and the Song of Solomon, and there's nothing about dinosaurs. Genesis. Exodus. Leviticus. Numbers. Deuteronomy. Joshua. Ruth.

I think of Grandma and her Quaker family, and I wonder why her mother named her Ruth. Ruth was not following tradition. She didn't remarry among her own family, but instead followed the mother of her dead husband, and the Bible doesn't say why. Grandpa says Ruth is a woman of principle, who is true to her husband even after death, that she is true to his spirit and he lives on because of her loyalty. But her dead husband doesn't procreate with her and doesn't end up in the line of Christ.

Yes, she stays loyal to his people, but what does that have to do with either him or his God? Is it loyalty to her late husband, or is her love for her mother-in-law, Naomi, thick with the love of self, heavy with the knowledge that women are their own people, that they are the true outliers, the underdogs, the forgotten ones?

She sticks with Naomi and lies on the floor near the bed of Boaz because she knows she has no inherent value. Her value lies in the comfort her body will provide for a man, and the knowledge that the fruit of a masterful performance can perhaps yield quality food and shelter for the offspring she will undoubtedly bear.

But Ruth's pride? Her strength? The triumph of her will is in her loyalty to her true people. And Naomi is her girl, her road dog, with whom she will live and die, about whom she says, *"For whither thou goest, I will go; and where thou lodgest, I will lodge: thy people shall be my people, and thy God my God."*

People say these words at wedding ceremonies, and I want to use my voice like a red pen and correct them for taking poetry out of context, for mixing metaphors, for misrepresenting a proclamation of independence as ordinary romance.

What did Grandma's mother want for her youngest child in Kansas? Did she want this Ruth to find a man in another land, a man in California who would be the world's leader during the Apocalypse? Did my great-grandmother know her daughter would use music to support the army of God?

Before her stroke, Grandma took me to the only opera I have ever heard. We went, just the two of us, she said, "because life can be tragic, but there's beauty in it." On the way, she told me about King Belshazzar and his dream about a disembodied hand that wrote words on a wall.

Picturing the words, which Daniel interpreted for the king, I said to her, "*Mene, Mene, Tekel, Upharsin.*"

And when she smiled at me, I repeated the words over and over, like a chant, as I thought about the message, which prophesied disaster: *Thou art weighed in the balances, and art found wanting.*

Grandma told me that when men hear predictions, they get afraid, but women get busy. Like Mother, she doesn't believe fear is useful.

Don't be afraid. Be competent.

Occasionally, the black phone rings, and Grandpa tells Mother she must bring us down the hill to the Field for church, so that we don't become feral. We put on our pillow-case dresses and brush our hair.

After church, I talk to Aunt Geraldine, one of the Field women who married my blood uncles. I tell her I read the whole Bible and some of it doesn't make sense.

She tells me about chiasmus, a structure common in poetry, which is all over the Bible. I have never heard of chiasmus and I want to write it down, but I don't have my catalog. I ask her how to spell *chiasmus*, and I repeat the letters over and over out loud. She says she has paper, and we write it down together.

She explains to me that chiastic structure is an ancient literary device used in Hebrew scripture and ancient Greek verse. When you use chiasmus, you are repeating things as if in a mirror. The second part mirrors the image of the first. It can look backward, but really, it's just another way of seeing.

She says the Bible is confusing sometimes because it's like poetry, and it says things in different ways to help us remember. Like how *the hour cometh, and now is, when the true worshippers shall worship the Father in spirit and in truth: for the Father seeketh such to worship him. God is a Spirit: and they that worship him must worship him in spirit and in truth.*

"All you have to do to understand anything is pay attention," Aunt Geraldine tells me, "and then write it down in a way that helps you remember. Writing is a way of loving things, like King David did in Psalms. He wrote prayers like poems. But you can also write poems like prayers."

Aunt Geraldine gives me a stack of paper, and I tie a red ribbon in each of the three holes so it makes a floppy book. She writes the word *Orisons* on the front and says I can fill it with my prayers. Now I won't have to find empty spaces in the Sears catalog anymore. Now I have space to write down everything that happens in our family.

"If it confuses you, write it down," Aunt Geraldine tells me, "and then change the order until it makes sense to you. And then write down what you think, all the details of what you think and feel, and circle back around to them until they make sense."

Then she tells me to wait, and she goes into a clubroom and comes out with a dictionary. She hands it to me without a word. I open it to a page she has earmarked with a little fold. The word *apotheosis* is underlined. I will write this down.

"May I keep it?"

She nods, and I slip it under my skirt, tucking it into the shorts I always wear underneath, before I scurry to the car.

We drive along Route 66, making our way through the valley, on our way back up to the Mountain, and I sit on my dangerous secret as Mother points out the Madonna of the Trail statue in Upland, near the Euclid Avenue walking trail. She tells us it's in honor of the American women who tamed this land. She has told us this before, but today she pulls the car over. I tuck the dictionary under the seat as we all get out and stand together under the statue and she tells us how the women from the Daughters of the American Revolution placed these statues across our nation.

I look up at the Madonna of the Trail, a thick gray woman in boots and a bonnet, her grim, determined face looking forward, a baby in her arms and a toddler pulling on her skirt, neither of which she seems to notice. Mother says there are many identical statues of this woman, representing all the pioneer women who sought religious freedom.

"Women know how to keep going," she says. "We were made to support men's dreams. They couldn't do it without us, and don't you forget that. God gave men visions and drive, but he made us stronger, so we can help them."

The Madonna of the Trail doesn't cry. Her face is firm and resolved, and she looks past her circumstances with a measured stare. I, too, am firm and resolved. Even Mother would tell you that.

I want to hear what the Madonna of the Trail thinks about the Bible. I stand beneath her, as if she is a goddess who watches over my journey. I feel like an idolater, looking up at her, even though I don't think she is a graven image and I'm not sure listening to her is the same as worshipping her. I want to hear her stories about settling this land, her experience with hunger and cold and fear.

I want to pull out the paper book I have created and write down all the words she would tell me. I picture myself writing down the Madonna of the Trail's story, looking for the apotheosis of her wandering.

"Your writing is yours," Aunt Geraldine told me. "You can use everything that happens to you, even the bad parts. Bad things are just conflict, and conflict makes plot. Write whatever happens, and use chiasmus if it helps. Just make sure the story ends the way you want it to."

I think a lot about endings and how to change mine. When we get back to the Mountain, I watch the boys from the Field working on the house they are building us. My bedroom sits right atop the San Andreas Fault, and as I watch, I anticipate being buried alive when the big earthquake comes.

Mother gets a phone call on the party line. She tells us Grandma knows someone who has a troubled grandson, an eleven-year-old boy who has many problems staying out of trouble in the outside world. "He will come live with us," she says. "He will be your new brother, so show him the love of Jesus."

We always have boys and men staying with us, so this isn't unusual, but I roll my eyes at my sisters.

Lizbeth slaps me across the face for my disrespect, taking

on the role of Dad, who isn't here. I ask her if she wants the other side too, and she slaps me again.

Loyalty, duty, respect, selfless service, honor, integrity, personal courage.

Pain is not something I acknowledge, and injury is not something I avoid. I stare at her, daring her to keep going. She says I deserve it.

I keep a lot of secrets, so maybe she is right. But our parents keep secrets too. Mother says Grandpa doesn't want us to have guns, but Dad has a .22 he hides under the seat in the Jeep, which he uses to shoot jackrabbits in Lancaster. Mother doesn't know or pretends not to know. I can never tell which.

Some of Grandpa's boys live with us during the build, and some of them will stay and live with us in the house after it's built. One of Grandpa's boys, who is twenty-two when he gets here, stays with us for years. He's nice to our dogs and nicer to us than we are used to. He does things our parents never have, like make us lunches and bring us blankets at night.

When he comes down the hall to tuck each of us in, he kisses our foreheads, which feels enough like love I want to reach for him and hold on. But I don't. I lie there, torn between need and fear. If I had a lock on my door, I would turn it, because I don't trust love and I don't trust kisses.

But he doesn't hurt me. When I'm shivering, he keeps me warm.

Still, some part of me doesn't trust him, because I have been somewhere like this before. I try to be brave, because

I am ten now and I aspire to be like the Madonna of the Trail: strong, even when it's cold and I'm hungry and tired and afraid.

So I lie on my back in my bed on the San Andreas Fault, eyes wide open, and let this man tuck me in. I stay awake for a long time, listening to his steps soften down the hall, picturing the earth cracking open and swallowing me whole.

Pinyon Pine

The pinyon pine has rigid 2-inch needles that are a pale gray or blue green, and small cones that resemble brown roses. In ideal conditions, this tree can grow up to 60 feet in height, but most are only 10 to 15 feet tall. They can be found in dry, rocky places from 3,500 to 9,000 feet elevation.

Almost all pines have edible seeds, but the size and quality of those seeds depends on the species of pine tree. Pinyon seeds are large, oil-rich, and nutrient-dense, and you can eat them raw or cooked.

The inner bark is also edible. To obtain it, use a knife or a stick strong enough to pound with a rock, and dig in past the outer bark to find the tender white meat underneath. You

*can eat the inner bark raw or roast it on your campfire. You
can also peel off the crystallized sap and eat it like candy.*

*Pinyon pine seeds are often called pine nuts, because they
are so nutritious. One pound of seeds contains over 3,000
calories.*

AUNT GERALDINE IS MARRIED to Mother's oldest brother,
Stephen, who is coming to the Mountain this week to read
the stars. Of course, he mostly cares about where the stars
were in biblical times, because he thinks he can prove the
relationship between the star of Bethlehem and the timing of
the Second Coming.

He says Grandpa is right about the end of the world being
nigh, and he has a lot of charts and graphs of constellations
and astronomical alignments and prophecies to prove this.
He thinks the night sky is a logical map that will lead him
straight to God.

But I think this logic is a wall, not a window. Like those
maps I drew in MGM, the center is what we value, and what
we see when we look outside of our center is determined by
our beliefs, not facts. I don't think Uncle Stephen will find the
verification he is looking for with those charts. Or at least, I
don't believe we will find what I'm looking for, which is proof
that God exists, or proof that he doesn't.

Uncle says the locations and rotations of the stars are
prophecies of the future. But I know they're just lights from
the past that took a long time to get here, and we're seeing
them right now because we are standing here on the earth

when that light reaches us. In MGM, they taught us there are about five thousand stars visible to the human eye, which is a minuscule fraction of the stars in the universe, and even the ones we can see are so far away we can never see them in the present. How is Uncle, who is certain the earth is only six thousand years old, going to figure out anything about a star that appeared on a night two thousand years ago? Even the writer of Revelation seemed to know that when we talk about stars, we mostly understand them as metaphors.

And there appeared a great wonder in heaven; a woman clothed with the sun, and the moon under her feet, and upon her head a crown of twelve stars.

Stars appear to travel across the sky from east to west. If you keep track of which direction they seem to be moving, you can determine which way you're facing. If you're north of the equator, you can use Polaris and your fists to determine your latitude. But in time, my siblings and I learn to identify Polaris in any season, on any night the stars aren't blocked by clouds. And we learn to walk miles in any direction in the dark and easily find our way back home.

If you know how to read the night sky, you know where you are and you can never be lost.

Which is saying a lot, because I'm always lost. Sometimes I think I have things figured out, but I don't. Grandpa changes his mind all the time, so it's hard to predict what will happen next at the Field. And there's a lot we don't talk about.

Silence is conspiracy, just as it is consent. In our family, we turn quiet when we are lost, and we have been trained to look up, not to one another.

Mother's family is big and complicated, and it has taken me a long time to figure out who is who, or even which of the boys from the Field are related to us by blood, because all of Grandpa's followers are our family, whether they are our blood relatives or not. And there are always boys living with us who we call family.

Since Dad doesn't have any relatives except faraway Grammie, our dad's family is our mother's family, which is the Field family itself. The four of us kids might be considered Dad's family now, but we're too young to be full members of the Field, so I'm not sure whether we count.

Mother has three older brothers and a younger sister, and except for her oldest brother, who shares Grandpa's name, all of them have the same names as the children in the Eriksen family, who were part of Grandpa's first group of boys. Mother doesn't understand why this confuses me, that they all have the same names and that we call them all Uncle, but Mother is never confused about anything.

She doesn't explain why her father named two of his blood sons after the Eriksens or why the two Eriksen brothers are more important than our blood family. She doesn't even think it's confusing that one of the Eriksens was present with her at my birth, while Dad was on the road with Grandpa. Dad says we are all paper cups and can be used interchangeably to carry the blood of Jesus.

All my blood uncles are interchangeable to me—tall, unkempt, loud, and brutishly brawlish, and all the ones who are married are married to very small women. Our mother's sister, Mildred, is also a small woman, standing under five feet tall, with little hands and little feet and a high, plaintive voice, which she uses mostly to try to convince Grandma we are trying to kill her.

But if I wanted to kill someone, it wouldn't be her.

Aunt Mildred is in her thirties and has always lived at home with her parents, maybe because she's safe from her brothers there, or maybe because she's safe from the world. But nothing is enough to make her *feel* safe. In the house she lives in with Grandma and Grandpa, all the windows are permanently sealed closed, and the outside doors are all fixed to spring shut and lock automatically. Their property is guarded by a wrought iron fence with spikes, protecting the driveway, and a Doberman named Lady, who barks ferociously.

But still, Mildred locks her own door against us and says we're trying to set the house on fire and we shouldn't be allowed to come over. No one in the family talks about this, even when I ask, but unlike her brothers, when she gets violent, she goes away for a few days. I think she goes to a doctor somewhere, because she comes back with pills, but no one will answer my questions about that.

Men don't get sent away when they're violent. Hurting people is something men are entitled to, because they are created to rule. At least, if they're big enough to get away with it. My uncles have been hurting me since my earliest memories of them, and I *pray without ceasing* not to get angry and fight back, because we girls were made from Adam's rib to be helpmates, and anger in women is a sin.

Vengeance is mine; I will repay, saith the Lord—which

means Grandpa can get mad or jealous and banish us, because he serves as God's proxy.

Before I knew which of my uncles are Grandpa's blood sons, I knew they must be related, because no one rebukes them for arguing in public, or being ferociously passionate about how to interpret the laws in the Old Testament. I can relate to being a middle sibling and wanting attention, so I recognize when they vie for Grandpa's attention, desperate for the respect he seems to grant only to Mother.

Grandpa's interest in Mother captivates me. Grandpa created an organization for boys, presumably because he has no interest in girls, but his older daughter is the exception. She is almost always an exception.

She could get Grandpa to make her brothers stop hurting us, but she pretends not to notice, even when we tell her. They chase us around, inside or out, around cars or tables or couches, and I scream when they catch me, but that just makes them call me a baby and tell me to toughen up. I think I'm already tough, but they find all the soft spaces of my body, twist them tight, and rub their whiskers hard against my skin until it welts up.

I know I'm not a baby anymore, because I have passed the age of accountability. Grandpa says eight is the age of accountability, which means you are old enough to go to hell. Before that, it's your parents' responsibility to teach you what's right and make you follow it, and if you don't, God will blame them, not you.

Jesus said to turn the other cheek. And now that I can go to hell for disobedience, I know I can't risk my soul to fight back. Just because someone hurts you doesn't mean they can't teach you something. I learn how to be quick on my feet, to capitulate to pain, and to be vigilant.

I love the word *vigilance*, and I love to think about how our *adversary the devil, as a roaring lion, walketh about, seeking whom he may devour.* If we resist him, steadfast in the faith, we know that the same sufferings are still experienced by our brotherhood out in the world, who don't have our resistance. But we also know that *the God of all grace, who hath called us to his eternal glory by Christ Jesus,* after we have suffered a while, will perfect, establish, strengthen, and settle us.

I memorized that a few months ago. Grandpa likes when we remember Bible verses, and sometimes he gives me Life Savers when I recite them to him.

When I'm at the Field, I know how to give people what they want. I know how to make myself small and listen without speaking. At the Field, we are cared for by the collective, so I've grown up in corners of clubrooms, buses, tents, and ballfields, paying attention to who is in charge and when and where.

I would plant myself under Grandpa's desk before his disciples filed in. I've learned who is in favor and who is out of favor, who to impress, who to avoid, who is likely to be excommunicated, and how to get information no one will tell me outright.

And I know how to find food. I know which trash cans are cleanest and who is likely to discard leftovers, and how and where I can retrieve them before the ants arrive.

Our life on the Mountain is different from our life at the Field, so I need new skills up here. And Mother is the key to knowledge. Whether or not she decides to teach me what's in her field notes, I will find a way to read them anyway and I will piece together the magic of what she knows.

I don't think Dad knows how much she knows, because we never tell him. She says it's not right for women to intimidate men, even when they're part of your family.

Yesterday, during one of her talks, Mother was pointing out a snow plant, which is the most obvious plant ever. It is red, and it is tall and almost always alone, rising out of the pinyon pine needles and other forest litter in the spring, looking like a bell. Snow plants are especially stunning when the snow melts, and you can see them flaming red against all the expansive white. I don't know how anyone doesn't know snow plants, but the guests on the walk seem genuinely surprised by them.

When she trains other docents, Mother talks to them in fancy language that reminds me of her violin music. I could listen to her talk about science for hours and never be bored. She talks about *inflorescence* and *parasitic roots*, about how the snow plant *parasitizes* the *mycorrhizae* of the *photosynthate* provided by the *conifer*. I make a map of the plants and write down all these words.

Mother doesn't consider herself our teacher. She says she's opposed to nepotism, but after I looked that word up, I don't think what she says is true, since she clearly benefits from Grandpa's nepotism. I suspect she's just uncomfortable being that close to us, since nurturing is a feminine value, and femininity is how sin got brought into this world. At least, that's how Grandpa sees it.

He says women ate of the fruit because we are weak, and we are always asking questions, and we don't like to obey or trust, so we must be forced to, by the wrath of God or man. He says he agrees with the Apostle Paul, who said: *Let your women keep silence in the churches: for it is not permitted unto them to speak; but they are commanded to be under obedience, as also saith the law.*

Sometimes I think Mother thinks if she acts like a man, she'll eventually become one.

Grandpa lets us live up here on the dirt, even though he always says the entire earth is the devil's domain. Sometimes I'm confused, because Mother knows all about the relationships earth creatures have with one another, which are complex and mutually beneficial to the ecosystem, and when she talks about these things, she never talks about the devil. Does Grandpa even know all the incredible intricacies of nature? Or that his daughter has designed a coloring book of the region, so that local children can color the various biota of the Angeles National Forest?

Of course, mostly Mother keeps these out of our hands. None of her own children have ever received one of her books, or colored in them, even as samples. But we know they exist, because we help her collate and staple stacks and stacks of these books, and sometimes we take them to the various nature centers, where they sell them and give the money to Mother.

No one in my family believes in school, at least not the Outside schools, which try to teach you subjects that will turn you into an atheist or a hippie. I'm lucky I got three years in El Monte's public schools. None of the leaders' kids go to school on the Outside anymore.

Mother isn't allowed to teach us, so sometimes we have to go down to the Field to be schooled with the other leaders' kids, who all congregate in Karelon Hall to learn together. We have less and less in common with them, but they are our people, so we spend time with them when Mother drives us down the hill, and we stay at their houses uninvited whenever we can't get back home.

When the Field followers come to the Mountain, our home is their home. So when Uncle Stephen comes up to study the stars, Mother says he'll stay with us. Whenever she says the word *uncle*, I stop breathing and I have to poke myself in my sternum to make the breath come back.

I try to picture which one of Mother's brothers is named Stephen. I don't know which are which from their names, only from their hands. All of them scare me, but to varying degrees. I will know which uncle arrives from the way he twists my arm, yanks my hair, or rubs his whiskers along my inner thighs, along the softest places of my body.

They call what they do to us "whiskerinos" and "Indian burns," rubbing their stubble across our faces and the insides of our arms and thighs, twisting our forearms in opposing directions until we call out, "Uncle." They say we need to be broken, like horses are broken, because *the spirit indeed is willing, but the flesh is weak.* I don't know if they want us to have stronger flesh or just want to break our spirits.

Uncle Stephen arrives on our mountain straight from the Field, with a backpack full of long scrolls of paper, which he unrolls across the wooden tables in the mess hall. He shows us the angles we will learn to measure between the stars, which will be visible from the clearing where we will go to start navigating.

I try to give him the benefit of the doubt. Everyone says this uncle doesn't have the charisma or God-given leadership skills of his father, but I think that might be the best thing about him. His cruelty might just be layers and layers of dross covering up a curious heart. Uncle keeps up with the latest discoveries in astronomy from the Mount Wilson Observatory, hoping to locate the star of Bethlehem. He says the Bible calls it a star, but it could have been planets lighting the sky, and the wise men, who were early astrologers, would have been intrigued by this and gotten to know God as a result.

When Uncle's hands are wrapped around a telescope, he doesn't look threatening. So I stay and learn to recognize geometry in the night sky. He has a strong stutter, so I watch his hands as he shows me how to point my fist in the direction of Polaris and measure the distance with my fists.

On our mountain, Orion is most visible during the winter, so we begin our training in the snow. Eight major stars make up Orion's body: Meissa represents the head; Betelgeuse and Bellatrix represent the shoulders; Saiph and Rigel serve as the knees; and Alnitak, Alnilam, and Mintaka, lined up in the middle, form Orion's belt. Uncle Stephen makes me repeat the names of all these stars, but once I do, he tells me the easiest way to start is by recognizing the Big Dipper, and if I understand this star pattern, I'll always know where I am.

From where we are, in fall or winter, we have to look close to the horizon for four stars shaped like a bowl and three stars that form its handle. Once we've found that, it's easy to locate the North Star. Just focus on the two stars in the bowl of the Big Dipper that are the farthest from the handle, and then imagine a line connecting them, extending upward. Keep following it, and you'll find the handle of the Little Dipper, the end of which is the very bright North Star, also known as Polaris.

If you can see both the horizon and Polaris, you can find your latitude by stretching your arm out in front of you toward the horizon and closing your hand into a fist, and then placing your other fist above the first fist and continuing to stack one over the other until one of your fists meets Polaris. Each fist approximates ten degrees, so with a little practice, you can count how many degrees separate the North Star from the horizon. This is how you will determine your latitude.

Of course, this is just a starting point, and you can practice it only from somewhere the horizon is visible, but as I begin to learn where I am in relation to each of these constellations and how they shift in relation to one another, I begin to think of myself as something that shifts in relation to the constellations I'm around too.

Even though the Field is full of boys, most of them won't stay to become our uncles, so I don't pay much attention to them. But I pay attention to Thomas, since he is one of

Mother's favorites, which means we see him a lot. He's also one of the least capable, and easy to trick.

Thomas doesn't know how to light a fire or put chains on our tires in the snow, which makes us laugh, something we don't do when our parents are around. Laughing at Thomas brings my siblings and me together. We find ways to trick him that make us feel powerful and strong. Unlike the other men who care for us, he seems to respect our knowledge, and he defers to our experience. We take advantage of this, as often as we can.

We tell him he has to put his head all the way in the fireplace to get the match to light. And then Becca turns on the gas Dad has recently installed, and Thomas yells as he jumps back. We ask him if he's hurt, and when he says, "Only my pride," we can smell his singed hair, and we find that hilarious. We pick milkweed and tell Thomas to eat it as a salad. And we pull the frozen sap off the pinyons and eat it like candy and then pretend to be sick, rolling around in the snow, like we're gagging and can't breathe.

We aren't nice children.

While Thomas is making dinner, we use trash-can lids as sleds and careen down the pine needles into the gully, pricking ourselves through our clothes. He doesn't stop us, because he has no idea where the edge is for mountain kids, and we all pretend there isn't one.

When he's ready to serve us dinner, we laugh and tell him that the milkweed is poisonous, then pull elderberries out of our pockets and eat a couple and tell him to put these on his salad instead. At this point, he doesn't trust us, which shows he has better sense than we thought he did. He doesn't know we have built up a resistance that he hasn't, so he would get sick eating them raw. He just knows that he doesn't know, and that makes us feel smart.

In the months Dad has been gone on the Trip with Grandpa, Mother's proselytizing has expanded to Outsiders. While she teaches visitors about the flora and fauna, she says she is really infusing her words with God's messages. In the meantime, we roam wild all summer, foraging for plants and practicing our survival skills, should the Apocalypse rain down upon us, and the blood rise to the horses' bridles.

Mother doesn't like when I sneak around, but I do it anyway, since she's stopped taking us with her on training trips. Today, I have intel that she's going somewhere new, so I hop in the back of the Jeep and lie down, and Mother unwittingly transports me into a syncline they call the Devil's Punchbowl.

She doesn't acknowledge me when I'm in the back, but when we get there, she waves at me, so I jump out and follow her. Mother introduces herself to the woman behind the counter in the nature center, and goes in the back to find whatever it is she came for. I'm not sure what to do, so I say good afternoon to the lady and start reading all of the plaques and signposts:

The Devil's Punchbowl is a unique 1,310-acre geological wonder where visitors can walk, hike or take a horseback ride on a 7.5-mile round-trip trail through a deep canyon formed by the runoff of large quantities of water from the higher San Gabriel Mountains. See spectacular up tilted rock formations created by layers of sedimentary rocks, or visit the Nature Center to learn about the native wildlife and park history. You can also explore the landscape of Joshua trees, California Junipers, Pinyon Pine, Woodland and Desert Chaparral shrubs while observing the variety of wildlife.

I learn that the canyon and its surrounding rock formations along the San Andreas Fault cover over a thousand acres of recently purchased public land. I ask the lady if Mother is going to be working here now, and she says, "I hope so."

Once Mother takes over the talks at the nature center, we are allowed to come along and survey the territory. As summer turns into autumn, my siblings and I hike and swim and learn to trap, pin, and label insects with Jarvis, the entomologist. We also commingle with the trepid wildlife, competing for bobcat and snake sightings, and we are elated, rather than afraid, when we see rattlesnakes, because they earn the highest point value. I think nothing of wrapping a California king snake around my neck like an elegant scarf.

The basin itself is three hundred feet deep at the vista point. After particularly harsh winters, when the hollow rock bowls are filled with the snow's runoff, we compete with one another by jumping off the highest rocks we can, plunging into the depths below.

Occasionally, as we are out on our escapades through the chaparral, we encounter stinging bugs and complain about the pain and welts. Jarvis teaches us that irksome insects play a valuable role in the biome, and I learn to appreciate the beauty of bugs. Even those noxious stinging and infectious insects, which antagonize humans, are intricately necessary to maintain the region's ecosystem.

When Dad returns, he doesn't like us tagging along with Mother, so he gives us more work at home to discourage the expeditions. But the Devil's Punchbowl is my favorite place to be, and I can almost always find a way to get back there.

Today we have come early, before the nature center opens, to deliver coloring books and collect payment. While Mother does paperwork in the back, the lady at the front desk lets me hold all the different snakes and lizards and tells me where each of them come from and how long they've been here.

I am excited to be here, wandering around the terrariums and cages, until the lady stops me and looks at me funny. She asks me what happened to my face.

I don't know what she's talking about. I reach up and touch my swollen cheek, and I imagine maybe it has begun to bruise. I tell her my dad didn't want me to come today, but I came anyway.

"Oh, honey," she says, with a tenderness that makes my skin crawl.

I don't know why this bothers her, but I don't want to embarrass or disappoint Mother, so I feign laughter, as if I am a silly girl. I make up a story that I think won't offend her. "No," I say, "I'm kidding. I ran into a tree branch yesterday when we were sledding."

She exhales in a way that sounds like a whistle, either because she believes me or because she's relieved not to have to inquire further. I make a note to avoid her, like I avoid everyone I've ever met who doesn't belong to the Field.

Before I leave, she hands me a pamphlet. "Here honey, this will tell you what you need to know." It's a government brochure about national monuments and forest service lands across our mountain range.

But I already know where I am on this mountain, even in the dark, because my uncle has given me the sky.

Snow Plant

The snow plant grows near pine trees, emerging dramatically out of pine needles and other forest litter—bright red, bursting like a fire.

Its five-petaled flowers are closely packed together into the shape of an elongated bell. The snow plant begins to grow above the ground in late spring, presenting a conspicuous contrast when there is snow.

Snow plants get their nutrition from fungi underneath the soil. The edible, vegetative part of the plant is its root, which has a texture and flavor similar to asparagus.

IT'S A FEBRUARY LIKE ANY OTHER on the Mountain: dark and cold, the ground thick with snow, glowing in all the places the moon lights up, making patterns in the shadows of the trees, like in *the valley of the shadow of death*. We park on Highway 2, near the ranger station, and we hike up the road, carrying our things, as we do every night since the snow started. I keep staring ahead of me, up each little hill, observing the way the dark of the night contrasts with the light of the moon, like a reflection in a mirror. Tonight it's silent, except for the coyote calls, which remind me we're not alone.

I've never felt alone since we moved here, not even when I'm the only one on the Mountain.

I remember the autumn, when the sounds of the crickets were like a chorus, and how back then, I would hike this road with ease. Now, every piece of me aches. My legs, my shoulders, my head. Is it the snow? Is it deeper than usual? I am falling behind, walking at the rear of our infantry line. My dad yells back, "Toughen up, Michelle! You're not a baby anymore. You should be leading us!"

I see a snow plant, and I sit down next to it, staring at its red head peeking up under a circle of light, like a halo on this patch of snow, and I wonder why anything so beautiful would choose to come out now. I ignore the sounds of my family and sit with the snow plant, curious and captivated. I don't know why I can't keep up anymore. I am committed to our calling, and I watch and I pray without ceasing; my spirit is willing, but my flesh is weak. I lift my face to feel the cold

of the wind as it stirs through the trees. The smell of butter-
scotch from the Jeffrey pines is palpable, reminding me how
hungry I am. And how far I still have to go.

Dad is yelling again, but it's from a distance, up the hill
now, so it's not as threatening. I get up and keep walking,
each step deeper in the snow.

Eventually, I see the house, the light flowing out from the
kitchen, illuminating thick icicles hung like art fixtures along
the eaves. Before I enter, I peel off my shoes and socks on
the cement portico, watching everyone else inside with their
hands around the fire. I look down at my weak body. Even in
the indirect light, I can see that my feet are covered in red dots.

I nudge up closer to the porch light and pull up my pant
leg, checking further. I observe that my shins are covered in
these same dots, but also bruises, so the color is muddled,
like an overripe eggplant. It is kind of pretty, but I know I am
vain for thinking this. Dad is right: I am a weak girl.

Like the uncles, Dad's hands are large and knotted, but
his are infinitely more capable. Dad is built for this mountain. He splits trees into logs, and he carries so many logs at
a time, I can't keep up with him. When we help carry logs to
the Jeep, it takes all of us kids to carry as many as he can.
Dad blows on logs, and fire appears, like it comes from inside
of him. And he can plant a field, mow a lawn, and crawl
under a car or a bus to fix it. And no matter where in the
country he is driving, he always knows where he is going.

But it's more than his hands. Every part of our dad is
capable. He doesn't think girls can be as capable, but I aim to
prove him wrong.

Back when we lived near the Field, I would sit on the counter in the bathroom while Dad lathered his face with Noxzema, heating the water until it fogged the mirror. I'd watch while he slid his razor across his white chin. Sometimes I would dip my fingers into the cream and softly, tentatively, quietly mold it onto my girly face.

Dad tolerated this in silence, without so much as a nod. One time, when he was finished shaving but before he splashed on his Old Spice with a violent shake, he took the blade out of his razor and handed me the empty shell. I carefully stroked my tender cheeks with the harmless metal, until each white row had vanished and I looked like a little girl again. Then I splashed my face with water and looked to him for approval. He didn't comment, but he held my gaze, and I felt something akin to respect. There was validation in the motions I had sequenced, almost in tandem with his, the ritual of manhood like a handshake between us.

Lizbeth tells me girls don't shave their faces, but I don't care. Our home is a man's world, where strength rules, and I am proud that I have stood next to him doing what men do.

My sisters say Dad looks like a bear, and they are frightened of him, of his gruff manners and his guttural growl. But I love watching his calm face in the mirror, as he meticulously removes every errant hair. I am never afraid when I can see my face in the mirror next to his.

But now I am afraid he won't like who I am becoming. I am ashamed of everything about my body, the way my chest is beginning to puff, the way the little hairs are growing between my legs, the way I am starting to smell like a girl.

Even if we shared a bathroom, Dad would never let me sit with him now. I am nothing like what a man should be.

Weeping may endure for a night, but joy cometh in the morning.

I climb into Becca's bed with her. She is already asleep, and her covers are warm from the heat of her body, so I curve my stiff, cold, aching hips around her soft, warm back. She squirms a little from the shock, but she doesn't ask me to leave, so I curl around her and fall asleep.

Before the sun rises, we hike down the road, and again, I am stumbling. I keep dropping the plastic bags I use to carry the things I will need while we're at the Field. I try to stay in front of Dad, who is now positioned last in our infantry line, pushing us from behind.

He is coming up closer now, and I can feel the heat of his presence. I notice his shadow first, so when he takes a swipe at me, I see it coming and duck. His fist catches the side of my face, mostly just my ear.

Now my ear is ringing, so I can't hear what he's saying, but I know enough to make myself move faster. I am lucky his hand is gloved and won't leave much of a mark.

On days we're at the Field, we roam anywhere we want and our parents don't ask where we are. Today, I climb up the grassy bank to visit the Washington family. I am not supposed to be here, because Mrs. Washington works on the Outside, in a hospital. I think it is nice of her to help sick people get better, but Grandpa says she is a heathen for not trusting God to water her lilies of the field.

Still, Grandpa is merciful and lets them live on the grassy

bank of the Field, since Mr. Washington has been working with Grandpa since he was a small boy.

Angela Washington, who is my age, is often home, looking after her three brothers, and preparing to care for the new baby who is on its way. She practices on her Baby Alive doll, which has its own special food she spoons into its mouth. When it starts to smell, she empties out the back compartment, like it's poop. I don't have dolls, but I used to do that for Danny, so I feel at home.

There is always someone to care for over here. Sometimes when Angela is busy with her doll, I make her little brothers toast with jam and serve it to them with milk in little teacups.

Today is shopping day. When Mrs. Washington arrives home, her three sons run out to help carry the bags. The oldest reaches in and opens a box of cereal, which he begins consuming with one hand while holding a bag under his armpit and another bag with his other hand. Mrs. Washington doesn't scold him for this. She just laughs.

I'm not sure whether she would care about my hunger if she knew, but she doesn't seem to even notice I am there. I'm sure I can wrangle some leftovers when they're through. I hold open the door, careful not to let the dog out, while the boys go back for more bags.

Now, every one of the boys has opened something ,and they are all chewing and chattering, their arms and hands and bellies full.

Angela is not eating. She waits patiently in the kitchen for all the bags to arrive and then helps her mother unload the food, expertly placing things on shelves in the pantry and refrigerator and freezer. I want to help, but I don't know where anything goes.

I watch, confused by the placement of each item, wondering how anyone could possibly have the money to buy so many different things. How does their mother know what to buy? How do they know what they are allowed to eat?

As I'm standing in the kitchen, trying to stay out of the way, drinking water from another household's cup, one of the boys runs into me and smashes jam against my long skirt. Mrs. Washington asks her daughter to go find me something to wear, so she can rinse out my clothes.

Mrs. Washington insists I take off my skirt so she can wash it, even though I tell her no, that she shouldn't bother. I try to go to the bathroom for privacy, but there's only one bathroom and there's always someone in it. Mrs. Washington says I should slip on the sweatpants under my skirt in the kitchen.

As I lift my leg to do so, she stares at the red spots on my ankle and asks me to stop and come to her room. I follow her to her bedroom, thinking she will give me privacy now, but that's not what she wants. She tells me to take off my skirt, and she touches my legs.

"How long have you had these petechiae?" she asks.

I shrug, because I don't know what she is asking.

"How long have you been like this? How long have you had these dots, these bruises?"

"It doesn't hurt that bad," I say. "I'm fine."

"How long?" she asks me again.

"A long time," I say.

Mrs. Washington drives me up the street a few blocks to a doctor she had worked with who practices near the Field.

The doctor says this is serious, that I am bleeding under my skin, that I may be bleeding internally. He writes something on a piece of paper and tells Mrs. Washington to call Mother.

Mother meets us at the doctor's office and sends Mrs. Washington away like she's crossed a boundary for which she'll have to pay.

Mother doesn't talk to me, but I follow her to the station wagon and climb in the front next to her. I never get to sit in the front. I feel like I've risen in rank, and I'm a little proud of this new status. But the drive is long and I get tired of being ignored. Mother is drinking coffee in a foam cup, listening to a cooking show and memorizing the ingredients to a crème brûlée, repeating the ingredients out loud over and over. She hardly ever cooks, so I don't know why she is interested in this particular recipe, but I pay attention to how to make it, so that I can surprise her someday.

When we get off the freeway and drive onto a street, there are so many cars we have to wait several rounds at each stoplight. While we sit in traffic, I watch the people walking, wishing I could get out and feel the ground under my feet, which always helps me get my sense of direction. We slow down to enter a parking garage, I see a sign on the side of the building, and for the first time I know where we're going: Children's Hospital of Los Angeles.

We move through the parking garage and into an elevator, through a hallway, and into a station where a nurse takes my height and weight and blood, and measures all sorts of things I've never had measured before. She asks many questions about my scars and bruises, and Mother answers them, mostly accurately, but even when she's inaccurate, I don't interrupt; children should be seen and not heard, especially around Outsiders. The Outsider nurse asks who lives with me and who cares for me, and Mother calls everyone family, even though our relations are by faith, not blood.

"Of course we don't hit her," Mother says.

I question who she means by we, but not out loud. It's true she has never hit me. Mother doesn't touch me at all.

The nurses search my body thoroughly and mark down what they see. I have a bugbite near the hair between my legs, and they apologize to me before they cut into it and take a swab. I think Mother will be angry at me for letting my hair grow there.

I leave my body and hover above it. I see the body of a girl being touched who doesn't want to be touched.

They ask me if I have started my period. I don't know what this means, but Mother says no.

After many tests, I am admitted as an inpatient to the hematology/oncology unit. They say they don't know much except that my platelets are dangerously low and that what I thought was a bugbite is really a single chicken pock. I have no other pox on my body, and no other symptoms of the virus, but they say I have chicken pox anyway, which could be dangerous to the other children in the ward.

So they put me in isolation. This means anyone who comes into the room must be gloved and masked and I can't have any visitors. It means I'll stay alone in the room until they know what is wrong with me.

I don't have pajamas, but the nurse hands me a tray. On it are light-blue pants, with little flowers and a drawstring, and a dark-blue top. Both are soft and worn, and smell a little like bleach, and I put them on, even though the pastel blue makes me think of the clothes I was wearing when Duchess died.

I look out my tenth-story window at the city, the endless gray asphalt, the tiny cars moving in all directions, like toys in the hands of boys. Everything looks so small, although I am not very big myself, which confuses me. I've never looked at anything from so high up in the sky.

Mother says it's time to get back to the family.

"Why are there so many cars?" I ask her. "Do they look like toys to you?"

"You'll be okay here," she says. "The nurses will take care of you."

"When you leave in one of those little cars, will I be able to see you from here?"

Mother doesn't seem to hear me. She uses the hospital room bathroom, and I wait for her at the window, still staring at the street until it becomes too blurry to see. I hear the toilet flush, and I realize then that I am wet with my own tears and I must clean them up quickly, with the hospital shirt. But it is thin and already obviously wet, and I am beginning to panic, because she will step out soon and see this mess I am making.

Which of course she does.

"Stop it," she says. "You're embarrassing me."

I choke back the voice that keeps wanting to come out of my mouth. I gag with the words I don't want to say. I fall on the floor, on my knees, and say, "Please let me come home with you."

"Don't be ridiculous. You have to stay here. You're sick."

"Please don't go."

"You're not a baby. Get in bed."

I don't stand up. I can't. I kneel next to my IV pole, hugging it like I'm a monkey in a zoo.

I don't hear Mother leave, but I hear the sound of the door as it closes behind her. I climb into the hospital bed. An overhead light is on, but I don't know how to turn it off. So I nestle my head under the covers until I am burrowed in so deep it's dark enough that I can pretend to be anywhere, like in a sleeping bag under the night sky.

I have blood tests so many times a day my veins can no longer support the needles. Eventually, they tell me I have an autoimmune disorder called idiopathic thrombocytopenic purpura, which they say I can call ITP, because it's easier. I repeat *idiopathic thrombocytopenic purpura* in my head three times and say it back to the doctor slowly and precisely, because I like the way it sounds coming out of my mouth. He says, "Good job. You have an ear for language."

My white blood cells are high, so at first they thought it was cancer. But it's really just a problem with my immune system, which is overreacting to a perceived threat and mistakenly attacking and destroying my platelets, which, I learn, are cell fragments that help blood clot. They say it may go into remission on its own, but for now, my platelets are so

low they can't even find enough to count. For now, I could
bleed to death from a scratch. So they want me to stay until
they can find out if there are more things wrong with me.

Night after night, I wait for Mother to return.

I get moved out of isolation into a room with a bald girl
named Sandra. Sandra is eleven, which sounds much more
grown-up than ten, but her father calls her a little girl and
tussles his fingers on her head, as if there is still hair there he
can play with. My father has never called me a little girl or
touched my head. Only Grandpa's boys do that.

Sandra is a year older than me, and everything I wish
I could be—tight and tough and brown—and I look up to
her for being here longer than me and knowing the ropes.
She knows how to talk to the nurses, and there is a girl
with stripes who comes in sometimes to bring her stuffed
animals or flowers. Sometimes they bring her library books.
I hope I live long enough to figure out how to get library
books.

Mostly, Sandra is quiet and talks only to her parents,
who are there nearly all the time. I watch them come and
go. Usually, her mom is there during the day and her father
is there during the night. Maybe they work different shifts?

But even when they aren't there, Sandra doesn't care what
channel the television is on. I don't know what to watch on
TV, so I ask her, but she shrugs. She stares off toward the
window, not at the screen. The window is on my side of the
room, so sometimes I think she is staring at me.

Sandra is thin and physically fragile in a way I think I,
too, will be someday. Maybe soon. In the evenings, when

her father is there, I am grateful I am farthest from the door, because when her father visits, he weeps.

I have never heard a man cry, so all I can think of is Jesus, and how Jesus wept.

I try not to look at Sandra's father when he weeps, but I can hear him, even when I push my face down into the pillow. I want to pull my curtain shut whenever he comes in, so that he won't feel bad, being watched. But if I get up to do that, he will see me. I wonder if he even knows there is a girl in a bed behind a half-drawn curtain, who can hear him cry and watches each of his moves, because he is the only thing moving in this room at night.

In the evenings, when it is darker outside than it is in our room, I stare at the window more than usual, drawn to the way it reflects me back to me, my body superimposed against the lights of the city, the motion of the streets. When I look outside, I also see myself, and I am reassured to see I am still there.

Mostly, I pretend to be asleep. My body hurts from being in bed all the time, but I am proud of how little I need to sustain myself.

Sometimes I have to get up because I need to use the bathroom. I hope I'm not bothering Sandra's father when I try to sneak into the bathroom, dragging my IV pole on wheels. But her father doesn't seem to notice me.

I am used to being invisible, so this doesn't surprise me. I can even hide in plain sight. Maybe this is my superpower.

They say I may die in here.

But I may not.

They give me bone marrow tests and blood transfusions, and sometimes I cry out. But then I remember how to hover above my body, like I learned to do when Grandpa's boys touched me, so I do that now too, and the pain feels like it's happening to someone who isn't me.

One day, the doctor tells me there is blood in my urine. They need to do more tests.

The nurse has given me special wipes to use the next time I go to the toilet. The wipe turns red, so I use another. That one turns red too. I have to be careful, because I am connected to an IV pole, and it's hard to move around in this small space.

I use toilet paper to clean up the blood that has dripped onto the floor, but mostly I am smearing it around. I throw the paper in the toilet, and it turns red. I am embarrassed; I know I'm not supposed to flush the toilet, but I don't want to leave a mess for the nurse.

Now that I am dying, like Sandra is dying, I wonder if my dad will come visit.

I can't walk out like this. There is blood on my gown now too. I push the square button on the wall.

The nurse comes in. "I'm sorry," I say. "I've made a mess, and I can't clean it." She looks at me with an expression I haven't seen before. Is it compassion? Relief? She asks me if this is my first period. I don't know what she is talking about. She asks me if I have ever bled like this before, and I say no, but I've never been dying before either.

She says this is good news, that they'll still run some tests, but chances are there's no blood in my urine at all.

She explains to me that this is my first menstrual period. It happens to all girls, and to all women, and it's nothing to be afraid of.

Is she talking about Eve's curse, delivered because she listened to the serpent? I ask the nurse if she means this curse.

"Oh, honey," she says. "There are a lot of stories about how we got here, but a menstrual cycle is just how our bodies get ready for babies. All mammals have reproductive cycles. It's not a blessing or a curse. Just nature's way."

She brings back a little white paper bag filled with disposable mesh panties and little cardboard boxes with individual sanitary pads in them. She helps me insert my first pad into the panties and shows me how to dispose of them when I'm finished. She tells me I am growing up, that I am becoming a woman. And then she tucks me into bed, like I am a little girl.

The nurse says good night to Sandra's father on the way out. Maybe he thinks I am asleep, or maybe he doesn't think of me at all.

She leaves the light on. They always leave the lights on in the hospital. Since it's never fully dark, you can never see the stars.

When she leaves, Sandra's father begins to pray out loud. He weeps. He begs.

But Sandra dies anyway, and I get a new roommate in the hematology/oncology unit of Children's Hospital.

I will have another roommate soon, and another one after that, and another one after that. Mother, who hardly ever visits and who doesn't really look at me when she does, says I will stay sick until our Lord cleanses me of my iniquity.

In the meantime, I find out how to get books from the hospital library, even though my parents don't like me to read anything but the Bible. The nurses give me a list to choose from, and my favorite is Jean Craighead George's *My Side of the Mountain*. The more time I spend with Sam on his mountain, the more I know my mountain is still with me.

Mother is embarrassed by me, and I am embarrassed by my weakness, and it's taking so long for me to get better; sometimes in her frustration, she asks, "How could you do this to me?"

I don't want to be doing this to her or to the Field, so I keep reading the Bible and pray without ceasing. I also read other books, but I don't want to make things harder on her, so I hide them when she visits.

Mother spends her visits asking the doctor and nurses questions about the treatments and trying to figure out the paperwork for how to process all the payments through the Ronald McDonald House, which is covering the bills for us. Mother says the world sees us as poor, but we are children of God, not man, so while we must pay *unto Caesar the things which are Caesar's,* we don't have need of their coins. Dad has never come to the hospital, so he doesn't have to worry about things out of his control. Mother handles all the particulars.

There is a lot Dad will never see and a lot Mother won't notice. They don't see the shiny floors or the colorful patterns on the nurses' outfits. They don't see how they clean up blood without anger, without reproach. They don't see the needle marks in the creases of my inner elbows or the bruises on my inner wrists, or the thick tape on the back of my hand that holds a needle in place there all the time, so that the nurses don't have to take it in and out. They'll never know how all these needles prick and protect me, like the layers of pine needles I used to sled on down the San Andreas Fault.

Scientists say the big one is coming, but my parents say you can't trust science. With faith as strong as a little grain of mustard seed, the Bible says we can move mountains. If that's true, there's no way our mountain is susceptible to anything God doesn't allow, even an earthquake.

And so maybe God will make me well. Maybe *the Lord will come as a thief in the night* and I will rise up out of this hospital bed and run back to the Mountain with renewed strength. I will *mount up with wings as eagles,* and I *shall run, and not be weary.* And I *shall walk, and not faint.*

Sugar Pine

The sugar pine can grow up to 200 feet tall and can live up to 500 years. It has slender deep blue-green needles with white tips, clustered in bundles of five. Its long, horizontal branches often droop at the ends from the weight of its 22-inch cones. It grows in elevations of 5,500 to 8,000 feet.

Like all pine trees, the sugar pine offers nutrition through its inner bark, needles, pollen, and seeds, but this one is known for the sweetness of its sap, which tastes like maple syrup. The seeds of a sugar pine have a nutty flavor, with a hint of resin. The nut, together with the shell, can be made into a nut butter. A sugar-like substance exudes from wounds made in the trunk of the tree and also from the cones. After this pitch dries and hardens, you can use it as chewing gum.

Mature sugar pines regrow after they've burned, using their extensive root system. Dormant buds are protected underground, and nutrients stored in its deep roots allow quick sprouting after a fire.

GRANDMA IS TEACHING PIANO AGAIN, so the little house is filled with the sounds of her students, most of whom play poorly. I know they play poorly because ever since I was a young child, Grandma has insisted I develop an ear for music, and now I am a snob.

Grandma taught me musical symbols on flash cards before I could read, starting with the symbols for quarter, half, and whole notes, the bass and treble clef, and sharps and flats. Now she expects me to know intervals—major, minor, augmented, and diminished—and how to express energy through tempo, understanding the nuances of adagio, allegretto, andante, larghetto, prestissimo, vivace, and vivacissimo, which mostly I do, because I love how those words dictate emotion.

There's a break from students in the afternoon, so I'm allowed to sit at the piano. I'm better at theory than practice, but I thumb through one of Grandma's hymnals and begin to play a melody, slowly and methodically, employing my best adagio, adding D, G, A, and B minor chords.

It's not as fluid as when Grandma plays it in church, even after her stroke, so I wait for her to tell me I'm playing it wrong, but she just keeps fiddling with her puzzle pieces at the table in the corner. I begin to sing softly, "*I come to the mountain alone, while the dew is still on the roses; and the voice I hear, falling on my ear, the Son of God discloses.*"

The words come out without my thinking. I see the old chapel and the sugar pine tree shading the small wooden benches. I have changed the printed lyrics from *garden* to *mountain*, because that is the only place I have ever felt God. I picture Grandma sitting at the small electric piano, Grandpa wildly swinging his arms, encouraging the boys to sing. I smell the pine and the dust and the sweaty bodies of the boys who have just hiked up the steep hill, sitting close together now, rubbing the flies from their faces as they sing, "*And He walks with me, and He talks with me, and He tells me I am his own, and the joy we share as we tarry there . . .*"

I haven't been home in a long, long time.

"We had a garden when I was a girl."

I am startled by Grandma's voice, and I stop playing.

"I used to sing that song in our garden when I would bring my mother the eggs from our hens. Jesus was with me then. He walked with me in the garden when I was a girl."

I wait for Grandma to continue, but she seems to have lost her train of thought.

I continue singing, "*He speaks, and the sound of His voice is so sweet the birds hush their singing; and the melody that He gave to me, within my heart is ringing.*"

I'm thirteen now, and I've been sick for thirty-one months, on and off high doses of prednisone as I rotate in and out of the hospital as an outpatient or an inpatient, as my condition loops through various cycles. When I'm doing well, we still drive to Los Angeles at least once a week so they can check my numbers, and when I'm bleeding too much, I stay there. But mostly I stay here, sleeping on the chair in Grandma's study, listening to the piano. This house is on the bank of the Field, and since there is no one more godly than Grandpa, if I'm here, God might spare me, like he spared Nineveh.

But Jonah was a man, and Nineveh was an exception. God doesn't have much of a track record for sparing women, so I'm not counting on it. During that whole Sodom and Gomorrah situation, Lot offered his virgin daughters up to the mob to protect the visiting strangers. But they weren't spared, and God didn't even spare Lot's wife, because she looked back. And I'm always looking back.

Every day, I think about things I shouldn't.

Survive fear. Survive with faith.

There was a time I knew how to feed myself on a mountain. There was a time I slept under the stars and knew how to find my way home.

For now, I am an invalid—invalidated—stuck here with Grandma and Aunt Mildred, neither of whom ever leave. I don't have a bedroom, because Grandma and Grandpa share the back one and Aunt Mildred has the front one. Grandma's study, where I stay on the fold-out chair, is really more of a hallway, since they've removed the doors. There are two open archways, one to their bedroom, and the other to the piano in the living room, so Grandma can easily walk back and forth in front of me, getting sheet music or workbooks.

Which also means Grandpa can watch me any time he wants. He says I got sick because I am like Jezebel, worshipping Baal and using my feminine wiles to ask questions and stir up trouble. He tells me I have to suffer the consequences of not being faithful to the great chain of being, in which God placed men at the top; my commitment should always be to Grandpa's leadership, and God will punish me until I remember that. He tells Grandma not to be fooled by me, because I'm manipulative, like Esther.

Esther is manipulative, but she's for sure a memorable woman, like Jezebel, and she has a whole book of the Bible named after her. Ruth is the only other woman who earned that, and truth be told, she was manipulative too. Most of the women in the Bible are vilified one way or another, but these ones are also feared, so there's worse things I could be. And anyway, Grandma loves Esther. She's been telling me the story of Esther since before I can remember. And Grandma isn't easily fooled by anyone.

Grandma was playing piano in churches and teaching piano when Grandpa met her. I give him credit for recognizing her value back then and snagging her while he could. There's no way he would have been able to build the Field if she hadn't earned the money they needed.

Grandma used to be president of the Music Guild in Pasadena, and she trained all sorts of people to become teachers. I've looked through her files of receipts and ledgers of income, and it's all meticulous. If she hadn't had that stroke when I was little, she could still be doing all that, instead of sitting here with me doing puzzles, stuck in this booby-trapped house, surrounded by a wrought iron fence with spikes, and doors that spring shut and lock automatically.

Grandma tells me we're waiting for my body to stop hating itself and for me to learn how to be a virtuous woman. She has taught me that a good woman knows how to earn money. In time, I absorb this and memorize all the verses from Proverbs 31.

To impress her, I play "Faith of Our Fathers," a hymn I know by heart, while reciting the Proverbs to her, doing my best to match the words to the rhythm, "*Who can find a virtuous woman? for her price is far above rubies. The heart of her husband doth safely trust in her, so that he shall have no need of spoil. . . . She considereth a field, and buyeth it: with the fruit of her hands she planteth a vineyard. . . . She girdeth her loins with strength, and strengtheneth her arms.*"

"Andante," Grandma calls out from the corner, and I pick up the pace, but just slightly, matching the words of Proverbs to the rhythm of the martyrs.

I wonder if Grandma notices the irony, but she doesn't comment, one way or another. Grandma used to tell me a good woman is like a tree, strong and gracious, shading everyone around her, keeping them from the wrath of the sun. I picture the sugar pine at the chapel, which seems taller than God. I want to be like that when I grow up.

"*She looketh well to the ways of her household, and eateth not the bread of idleness,*" I sing. "*Favour is deceitful, and beauty is vain: but a woman that feareth the Lord, she shall be praised. Give her of the fruit of her hands; and let her own works praise her in the gates.*"

When I finish playing, Grandma stays silent. I didn't expect applause, but I'm a little impressed with myself and disappointed that she isn't more pleased.

"When did you become a virtuous woman?" I ask her.

She positions two puzzle pieces into her landscape instead of answering. I feel bad for bothering her, but I really want to know, so I try again. "Did you have to give up being a Quaker to become a virtuous woman?"

"No," she says, almost before the question leaves my mouth. "No, I left the Friends Church to honor my husband, because God made Adam first."

She puts in another puzzle piece, and I close the lid on the keys of the piano, assuming the conversation is over.

"But the Lord works in mysterious ways," she says, "and my family did many good things for this country, and they were always open to change, so that's one thing you can learn from the Friends. I learned to be a virtuous woman by playing music, because my father thought it would be good for the church to come together, and music sustains us in difficult times."

When I think of the rest of my family, my heart hurts. I haven't seen them in a long time. Dad would approve of my learning piano, if I could earn money with it. He says women should all learn a trade, because you can never count on a man.

When my body is better, I will make money for my family too.

It's hard for Dad, trying to provide for us without being able to work for money outside the Field. But Mother says it would disappoint Grandpa if either of them worked for

Outsiders, because he wants them to trust him to provide. She says she would never do anything to disappoint Grandpa, which I think is another way of saying he can't be disappointed by what he doesn't know. Selling coloring books and giving nature tours and speaking in church don't count as work because Mother says they're not work, and that's that. But I don't know how we'd survive without the work she does.

"Does a virtuous woman ever disappoint her parents?"

"I did," Grandma says.

ON MY NEXT VISIT to the hospital, I get to see Dr. Shore, who is the head of hematology/oncology. I like my weekly visits with him, because he looks at me when he explains things and he answers all my questions, no matter what they are or how long it takes me to formulate them. I ask him if my body hates itself. He says the body isn't conscious like that. It's autonomic, he tells me, just doing the job it's meant to do. In fact, he says, my spleen and liver are doing a spectacular job filtering out old and damaged cells and helping to control the blood cells that circulate in my body, as the lymphatic system defends the body against infections through a network of lymphatic vessels that carry lymph, a clear, watery fluid that contains proteins, salts, and other substances, throughout the body. My body is producing extra antibodies, and these antibodies are coating my cells, and my lymphatic system is triggered to destroy whatever is covered in antibodies. Which includes all my platelets. No matter how many platelets my body produces, my spleen and liver clean them all right out.

A normal platelet count is 150,000–400,000, but without prednisone, my count is always below 5,000. My platelets are usually so low, they count them by hand, but even then, they can't see enough to get an accurate count, so they just say they're under 5,000.

When my platelets are under 5,000, Dr. Shore says it scares him, but it's the only time I feel free. I would rather be in the hospital than on the folding chair in my grandparents' study.

Dr. Shore says my body is protecting itself from what it perceives as threats, and we just need to trick it into relaxing, so that it will stop putting up defenses against invaders that aren't real.

I think a lot about invaders. Everyone in Grandpa's household is afraid of invaders.

I walk around the house at night, when the only creatures who move around are the dogs. Aunt Mildred's door is always locked, even when she's in the bathroom. I've checked hundreds of times, and I've never yet found it unlocked. I think it springs shut and locks automatically, like the front door. Aunt Mildred wears the key around her wrist, so that she always has it available.

One by one, I check every window in the house, climbing up on a chair to check the taller ones, even though I'm not supposed to climb on anything. Every window is sealed shut with paint, and maybe with wood glue under that. I pick away at it sometimes, but I can't pick away enough to get any of the windows open.

I pet all the dogs, even though I don't like them. It doesn't seem fair to withhold affection from a creature for doing what it takes to survive. Lady has bitten me more than once, but I know that's what she's been trained to do when someone comes in from the Outside.

I'm never really outside anymore, so her barking doesn't scare me. Lady is out there barking now, protecting us from invaders we can't see. Sois is old and incontinent, and can't play piano anymore, because she can't support herself on her hind legs. She just lies around looking sad, like me.

I'm supposed to teach Little One to play the piano now. He's a toy poodle puppy they got to replace Sois. But there's no point. I won't be in any more circuses, now that I'm sick. And anyway, Little One doesn't look like a dog. He looks like a puppet. No one's going to be impressed with that.

Maybe I will be eaten by dogs, like Jezebel was.

I don't know why everyone says all those horrible things about Jezebel. I've read her story over and over. How was Jezebel significantly different from Esther? What was Jezebel doing but being loyal to her people? Is it because she painted her face?

Just because Mordecai, or whatever other man they claim wrote the book of Esther, doesn't mention Esther using makeup, doesn't mean she didn't do that and more, so that the king would choose her as his queen, giving a better chance of her offspring surviving for generations, eventually leading to Jesus. All over nature, plants and animals use color as a reproductive strategy. Why shouldn't we?

I don't have anyone to talk to about my opinions. I can't even take the dogs outside to relieve themselves, even when Grandma is busy teaching, because I'm not allowed to open the front door. No one here seems to notice that Sois and Little One pee and poop all over the carpet. I pick up the poop with toilet paper and flush it down the toilet, but the pee soaks in and I can never get rid of the smell. One of the wives from the Field comes in and cleans up the house twice a week, and I tried to tell her, but she said I'm blaspheming.

I go through every book on Grandma's shelf. One day, I find *Grandmother Remembers: A Written Heirloom for my Grandchild*. I thumb through the pages of personal questions, beginning with memories of early family life. Most of the lines are blank. Grandma has had this book for years. I wonder if it's apathy or a reluctance to tell that has kept her from filling in the blanks. So many pages, so many disparate questions:

> *My favorite pet while growing up was* _____ .
> *My mother's full name was* _____ .
> *For dinner we used to sit* _____ .
> *I always hated it when* _____ .

Though Grandma has made little effort to preserve such seemingly trivial information, I flip through anyway, thinking that what I do find will be all the more pertinent. I want clues to Grandma's past before Grandpa, to the time when she was a little farm girl growing up in Kansas, before the Depression, before she came to California for better opportunities, and had the misfortune of meeting Grandpa.

Under the heading "How the World Has Changed Since I Was a Little Girl," most of the sections are filled out.

Grandma's handwriting is tiny and neat, and her words are in pencil, as though she thought she might want to change her mind.

> *When I was a girl, we didn't have* telephones. *They have invented* televisions *since I was little. I think a woman president would be* a no-no for me. *The thing I am most glad to have now that my mother never had is* a washing machine. *The thing I am least glad to have is* all the talk about sex.

I read that line again. With all the crazy contraptions of modern-day life, Grandma is least happy about *sex*?

> *Women today are* independent. *Movies today are* rotten. *If I could, I would go back to a time when* people didn't talk so much about sex. *I still like the old-fashioned ways of* courting. *If I had to give one message to the younger generation, it would be* don't have sex.

Grandma teaches me all about the seven seals of the Apocalypse, so that we will be prepared for the end of times. She teaches me about the sixth seal, the *great earthquake*, the sun *black as sackcloth of hair*, and the moon *as blood*. She makes me repeat to her about how *the stars of heaven fell unto the earth, even as a fig tree casteth her untimely figs, when she is shaken of a mighty wind*. And she asks me, when *the great day of his wrath is come*, how I will *be able to stand*.

I describe to her how the heavens will depart *as a scroll when it is rolled together* and how every mountain and island will be *moved out of their places*. *And the kings of the earth, and the great men, and the rich men, and the chief captains, and the mighty men, and every bondman, and every free man* will hide themselves *in the dens and in the rocks of the mountains* and will say to the mountains and rocks, *"Fall on us, and hide us from the face of him that sitteth on the throne, and from the wrath of the Lamb."*

She approves of my knowledge, but I think she may have it wrong: The people in the mountains won't want the rocks to fall on them. The people in the mountains will know the rocks are their refuge. If I hide in the mountains to avoid God's wrath, I will be safe.

The Mountain is a refuge. The Mountain is my home.

Grandma says I'm staying here because this house is protected. But I don't think she knows what protection is, what it feels like not to be afraid. Grandpa has warned her about the outside world for decades, filling all our minds with graphic tales of the rapes and murders men commit against women, making them sound commonplace and inevitable, without the help of the Lord and constant vigilance.

I stay up at night and memorize the passages Grandma asks me to. The words and images are heavy, but I am used to carrying heavy things. She pumps me full of piano theory and Judeo-Christian history to make me strong, but this knowledge doesn't feel like sustenance. The sustenance I rely on is from the Mountain, which has made my mind large, open, like the night sky, where there is room for paradox.

I am not on the Mountain, but the cadence of the Mountain is with me, narrated in the language of the King James Bible.

Jonah didn't obey God at first, but in the end, Jonah gave in and did as he was told, and God showed mercy to the people and saved Nineveh.

Grandma likes the story of Jonah. Unlike Grandpa, she believes that at the end of the world there will be mercy.

Dandelion

The dandelion has leaves with jagged edges like lion's teeth, which is how it got its name, derived from the French, dent de lion. Its yellow flowers bloom most of the year, at any elevation.

Its young leaves can be enjoyed raw, providing vitamins A and C, potassium, and calcium. The 1-inch section between the lower leaves and the upper roots can be eaten as a vegetable. If you cook dandelion leaves, they taste similar to spinach. If you grind, roast, and boil the roots, they taste like coffee.

Dandelions grow in almost any damp place and have saved many people from starvation. The biggest risk when *eating raw dandelions is the array of pesticides used to kill them. When you forage for dandelions, remember that poisoned fields are your greatest threat.*

WHEN GRANDMA GETS THE PHONE CALL, I am listening, as usual. She holds the earpiece far enough away from her head that I hear the words. She drops the receiver like she's been burned. I pick up the dangling phone and say thank you to Mr. Eriksen before I hang it back on the wall. Grandma looks dizzy. Our world has tilted, so it's reasonable for her to be vertiginous. I look at her and am grateful I have the language to diagnose the situation and the training to move forward without fear or hesitation. I was born for such a time as this.

My whole life I've been told that when Grandpa is taken to heaven, the world will end, but having memorized all the symbols in the book of Revelation, I think this is only the beginning.

I ask Grandma to sit down at the table, and I bring her a glass of water. Then I walk out the front door, letting it spring shut behind me. I run down the bank to the Field, where I see our people crying, some of them alone on benches, or gripping the rail of the stairway like they can't hold themselves up. Some of them are huddled in groups, their heads bowed, praying. Some are silently tearful. Others are wailing. I dig my fingernails into the soft spaces of my inner wrists to get myself to cry, but my face remains dry.

Grandpa wasn't supposed to be mortal. He said he was never going to die. Grandpa said Jesus would sound a trumpet

and he would rise up along with the saints as they were summoned whole from their graves.

When I was little, every time I couldn't find my parents or
other leaders, I thought the last trumpet had sounded and I
had been left behind. Grandpa had said then that the world
would end in 1977, after the signing of a treaty with Israel,
but he later said that because of the Field and our righteous-
ness, God had decided to spare the world a little longer, giving more people time to turn from their wickedness before
they were condemned to spend eternity in hell, where there is
weeping and gnashing of teeth.

Of course, Grandpa also said that he would live to be five
hundred years old, like many of the prophets before him, that
he would usher us into a new era, and then, when God was
ready, he would take him up to heaven in a whirlwind, as he
did Elijah. But human time is an illusion, so it's difficult to
gauge how much time we have until the next stage.

All the things Grandpa prophesied must now come to
pass. I look up at the sky for signs. It won't be long now until
the sun grows dark, the moon turns bloodred, war breaks
out, and blood rises up to the horses' bridles.

Mr. Eriksen puts out a call for Grandpa's blood grandchildren to meet in the pavilion to decide our next course of
action now that Grandpa has gone to be with our Lord.

I don't want to go into the pavilion. I don't want to hear
what they have to say.

Grandpa created our world, and he is the source from
which it flows. We are like fish in a pond, and he is the water
we swim in. Our gills know how to process only the oxygen

of his words. Maybe he will resurrect in three days. I don't know how else we will function, or where we will go if the water dries up. I picture us all flopping and flailing around on the ground, unable to breathe without the water in which we were given to swim.

I am a girl on the verge of womanhood. I have been summoned to the pavilion of my dead Grandpa, who is maybe modern Jesus for whom the trumpet will sound and the skies open, and I don't want to go under the umbrella to wait for what's next.

The leaders say Grandpa was God's final prophet, and now that he's dead, we don't know how long we have until the world ends, but we must stay strong. They say an angel took him, and I picture this, his bed lit up like an explosion—*and, lo, the angel of the Lord came upon them, and the glory of the Lord shone round about them*—and I am surprised the staff wasn't killed for seeing the back side of God.

They will say we are the light of the world, that we need to hold up Grandpa's standards, that we may yet be able to stay God's angry hand. But all I can picture is Grandpa's big black boot kicking Danny in the head for falling asleep during devotions.

And now, the world will be brought to an end, and we will have to hide in the rocks of the mountains. I am good at hiding and I am good with rocks, and I'm glad I won't have to go back to the hospital, but I've made it so far, all the way to my teens, and now I won't have the chance to grow up and kiss a boy.

I don't count what Grandpa's boys did to me when I was little. I know it made me unclean and God won't spare me now that the world is ending, but still, it's not the same as kissing. It doesn't count as my first kiss because I never kissed them back. Girls have to do what boys say at the Field. That's God's will. It's part of being a virtuous woman, learning to be a vessel for a man's seed. Grandma had to do it for Grandpa, just like I had to do it for Grandpa's boys. They say God made women to serve men.

Even though my platelets are still very low, I go back to the Mountain with my siblings to wait and to pray. Our house is quiet. None of us cry. Seven days pass without Mother talking. We eat handfuls of peanuts from the cans of government subsidies Dad picks up, and we wait for the sound of the trumpet.

I stand in the doorway, watching Mother choose her clothes for the funeral. She hates when I watch her, but she doesn't tell me to go away. She doesn't tell me anything at all.

When we lived at the old house in the valley, I used to stand in the kitchen with my siblings, watching my mother gather her things to depart for the evening, and I would ask her softly to stay, to please stay. I would have the sad face on, a look of need, and her body would harden as she turned to look at me.

"Stop it!" she would hiss in a whisper, her face contorted in controlled anger.

I would close my eyes and pull the emotion in like a syringe, softening my face before the tears could emerge.

Watching Mother prepare for the funeral, I take a deep breath. Nothing. I have swallowed the sadness, and it lingers in my belly like a dead animal waiting to rot. My face shows nothing. I am sure of this from the way my mother turns away again, that I have managed what she most respects and demands. I don't show my cards.

She has told me since I was three that the worst thing a girl can ever do is cry for herself. The goal of womanhood is not to shed a tear, for either physical or emotional pain. Childbirth will bring pain, but you can't let it get to you, she says. The Ticuna Indian girls don't cry, she tells us. Not even when they are eleven years old and everyone pulls out all their hair until they're bald. They don't cry even then. The community circles around the girl, torturing her, but she can't show fear, can't lose her composure or show any signs of distress. This is what it is to be female, my mother says. And when the Ticuna girl's hair grows back into fullness, she can get married. That's the consolation. Marriage. That's how we become women. I want to crawl back into Mother's stomach so she can't push me away.

"You have nothing to complain about," Mother commonly says. "You have it good. Your life is easy."

No one has pulled out my hair in handfuls, it's true. It's also true that things are easier without Dad, easier when he's gone traveling with his boys. It's true that his rage and random violence are more difficult to manage than her predictable whispers and the tightness of her lips pursed in displeasure. It's true that I have very little to fear from her, as long as I keep my emotions and my needs to myself. As long as I don't ask for anything, I can remain in her presence. What's important is to meet other people's needs and to be polite. Especially to Grandpa's boys.

As I watch Mother get ready for Grandpa's funeral, I think about Grandpa's boys. I can't get the visions out of my head. I remember how Frank used to hold on to the molding of the doorway like a spider—cavalier, appearing disinterested, like he had nothing better to do. If there was an earthquake, I think, he would have been holding on tighter, bracing himself for imminent disaster, but it's obvious he didn't have to for me. Clearly, I was not a threat.

I hover above my seven-year-old self, lying on Lizbeth's bed, watching Frank eye me with his half grin and his wide eyes like headlights. He is one of the boys Grandpa used to coach, who is well past the nineteen-year-old cutoff, making him too old to play. Mother says Dad asks these boys to watch out for us while he's on the Trip and that we should be nice to them and grateful that they care for us, because they're not bound by blood.

I see a little girl lying on the thin red bedspread, her bottom peeking out under her dad's old football jersey, knees bent, calves up, ankles crossed. To Frank, most of this is hidden behind my shoulders and head, which I keep erect and on point. I look closer. I see Frank stare at me with a predatory look I have seen before. I am perched up on my elbows, watching him linger, positioning myself so that he can only see my face, which betrays nothing. I am used to not being in control. Lizbeth, Becca, and Danny share this room with me, and it feels arbitrary and random who might pounce and when. I don't face away from the door, not now, not ever.

But my siblings aren't here in this memory, so I try to smile and be polite to Frank, even though I don't know what he's been protecting me from when no one is around, or what he sees when he watches me, when he smooths the baby-blond wisps of hair away from my cheek and runs his hands along the length in back, pets me like a kitten, demure and soft to touch.

I know Grandpa asked Mother to cut my hair, but she hasn't yet. Women don't have long hair where I come from. Maybe I am too young for her to see me as a woman, so I am not significant. Her own hair is dark and coarse and shorn tight like a boy's. Maybe she is proud of herself for producing what she is not, or maybe the blond hair and light eyes remind her of her husband, a man who still loves her in a way no one else has.

I don't know. She's never here. Dad is on the Trip for the next ten weeks, and if I were a boy and eight, Mother says he would take me. But for now I am a girl and seven, and Dad already has his sights set on Danny as his athlete, and I keep thinking that maybe Danny won't have the moves, and Dad will reconsider and train me instead. That's my plan, to get trained by Dad, so that I can compete in the world and get out of here. I know we can't always be with our parents, but when Frank is in charge, home is the worst place anyone can be.

All Grandpa's boys will be at the funeral, except Frank. I haven't seen him in six years, but no one has ever told me why.

Back then, Mother said girl babysitters are no good, because they coddle us and make us weak. She called all of Grandpa's boys our brothers, but they aren't in the pavilion when we're called in and they won't get to come to the front of the line with us to see Grandpa's body. Whether Mother admits it or not, there is obviously more than one kind of brother.

The funeral is in the pavilion, and when we get there, long lines of people are waiting to sign the guest book and look at his body before they sit down. At first, my siblings and I stand in line too, waiting for our parents to come back from wherever they are and join us. I look at the black suits and the black dresses and all the black stockings and shoes, and then I see the yellow dandelions in the grass, so bright in contrast. I want to pick one and blow a wish for Grandpa to come back, but Dad would get mad. He says spreading the seeds of dandelions is irresponsible. He has a right to say this, because he is the one who has to buy weed killers to get rid of the dandelions in the fields, and the last thing he needs in this world is more work.

Mr. Eriksen sees us and pulls us out of line and takes us up front with our blood cousins, so that we can see Grandpa's body. Our parents have somehow already funneled through and are seated in front.

Grandpa is lying on his back, his hands folded over his chest. I've seen him wearing that gray suit before, but nothing else about him looks familiar. His face looks like wax, like the plastic kind with fangs we put in our mouths when we play a villain in our plays.

But Grandpa couldn't be wearing fangs, could he? He isn't smiling in his coffin, so it's hard to tell, but his lips aren't quite closed, and as I look closer, I see he doesn't have teeth at all. Where are his teeth? Why doesn't Grandpa have teeth? And is that lipstick? Why is he wearing lipstick? There's no way he's rising from the dead looking like that.

Grandma is wearing her formal dress, which is black and has lace on the collar, and I can tell she has her girdle on. She is clean and neat, and her face is calm, like Mother's.

I want to ask Mother why we need more brothers, and why I'm the only one who got sick, and why the Monitor caught on fire, and why Grandpa lied to us about living to be five hundred. I want to ask her what happens to the wild animals she tracks, why they don't die from her touch. I want to ask her if not touching me has kept me wild, and if that's what she secretly wants for me, to stay that way.

I want to be like Esther, who knew the king forbade questioning and yet *who knoweth whether thou art come to the kingdom for such a time as this.* Esther says if she perishes, she perishes and she and her servants cook a meal and invite the king's friends, and she wins his heart and saves her people.

Not that Esther has many choices. She doesn't choose the king. The king chooses her, because she is young and a virgin, but then she manipulates the king with her words and tricks him into saving her people.

We are seated in front. My mother is wearing a hat, so it is hard to see the choir of children over to the left.

The children are singing: "*Feed My lambs, tend My sheep, over all a vigil keep; In My name, lead them forth gently, gently, as a loving shepherd of the Lord.*"

People are still shuffling through in a line, looking at the coffin. One of the aunts who married our blood uncles has a brother who is a Quitter. He stands in front of Grandpa's head and breaks into sobs. He wraps his arms around the coffin and drops to his knees and wails so loudly I think someone will ask him to leave.

I look at Mother, who is looking at the singing children. Her face is solemn, and she is quiet. Mother doesn't acknowledge displays of emotion, and she turns her head from Sodom. She and Dad have taught us that men who show emotion are what the Bible refers to as sodomites.

Some of the women are wearing jewelry—bracelets and necklaces, and even clip-on earrings. Grandpa would call them harlots, if he were alive to see them.

Sometimes I think about using an ice cube to chill my earlobes and piercing them myself with a needle. Esther might have done something like that. Of course, I would burn the needle in the fire first, to prevent infection. Mother says if I ever defile my body by dyeing my hair or getting piercings, I will be dead to her. But I have a lot of hair (which she's never brushed), and I don't think she would even notice.

When I think about jewelry, I think about Frank. Six years ago, I told him I wanted a jewelry-making kit, and he said he would buy one for me. I waited and waited, but he never did. I wanted to make jewelry that would protect me, jewelry like Wonder Woman's bracelets, jewelry that will ward off hostile invaders. I don't know how I will make this jewelry work, but I know if I can create pieces myself that I will make them strong, durable, and pretty, and they will be sufficient against whatever weapons Frank can use on me.

Frank didn't really use weapons, though. He was nice to me. While my parents were at the Field training up young leaders in the way they should go, he sent the other kids out-side with Big Stick Popsicles and said I was special, so he had brought me something even more special, a fifteen-inch Marathon bar—a braided chocolate-covered caramel bar I had never seen the likes of, and this was the largest version available—and he said he would sit on my bed and read to me while I ate it.

I sat cross-legged across from him, far enough away that he could barely nudge me with his feet, and I sucked on that gooey chocolate bar for an hour, making it last while he read to me from *Strong's Concordance*, and I would quote back the passages from the Bible I had memorized. He said I was as smart as a circus monkey.

I asked him to read to me about Esther, because Grandma said she was so beautiful and clever the king gave her any-thing she desired. The king sought her out from all the women in his harem. Her uncle Mordecai and God brought her to the kingdom *for such a time as this*. I loved the sound of that, loved the way Grandma imitated the drama of Esther's words, how she got the king to save her people, the Jews.

I remember Frank reading it to me, and I think there must be hope in revealing the truth. Esther had hidden from the king the secret that she was a Jew too, but she revealed it now, when she needed to. If the king were to kill her people, as he planned to do via military edict, he would have to kill her too, she told him. According to law and tradition, he should have killed her for deceiving him, and for making a request of him unsolicited, and, of course, for being a Jew in the first place. But he had come to love her, so he raised his scepter so she could enter safely and make her request of him.

Frank runs his hands along Dad's jersey, past my waist, and removes my panties. And I recite the verses and keep thinking, *The king forgave Esther's deception and told her he would honor her request, even if she wanted half his kingdom for herself. He would give her half his kingdom even though she lied by omission. And he saved her life, and all of her family, and her whole tribe of people.*

I don't know what will happen if I tell Dad about the way Grandpa's boys touched me, if I tell him what they do when he's not here. Maybe he knows. Maybe Mother told him. I try not to think about this. I try not to think about why they only came to our house when they knew he wasn't there.

All I know is that when I grow up, I will have the courage, like Esther, to tell someone the whole truth. And maybe someone will love me someday, and I will know he loves me by his forgiveness, and *I will go in unto the king, which is not according to the law: and if I perish, I perish.*

I don't tell Mother I would die for her love, but I don't think it would surprise her if I did. There are worse things than death, and that's what she has prepared us for with all those stories from *Foxe's Book of Martyrs*—to be willing to die for her and what she believes in.

The love of the God we believe in isn't warm, like a blanket or a fireplace. It's not even like a wildfire, the flames of which can be fanned by wind or quenched by rain. The love

our God gives us is more like a chemical burn, with no temperature control or natural abatement system. The searing
of our God is put inside of us, like rounds of chemotherapy,
aiming to kill off all the bad parts and leave the good alone.

Wild Rose

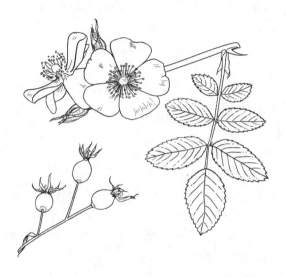

The wild rose grows on a sprawling shrub with curved prick-les and an alternating pattern of 5 to 7 leaves on each stem. The flowers look like cultivated roses but smaller, with only 5 petals, white to pink. They bloom May to August, with the fruit following the flowering.

The "hips" are the fruit of the rose, the round portion that grows just below each flower's petals. They remain on the shrub throughout the winter and spring, providing excellent foraging outcomes in times of scarcity. Both wild and culti-vated rose hips are edible.

Rose hips contain the seeds of the rose plant. They are usually red to orange, but in some species they can be dark *purple or black. You can eat them raw, like a berry, or boil them into tea.*

Rose hips contain more calcium, phosphorus, iron, and vitamin C than oranges. They can quench thirst and have been used to boost immune function, as well as increase urine flow and blood flow to the limbs.

GRANDPA HAS BEEN DEAD for three months, and Mother has finally agreed to let the hospital take out my spleen. Dr. Shore says a splenectomy might not work, but nothing else they have tried is working, so it's probably worth a try. He tells me they will need to pull back my ribs to get in there and that the healing will take some time, and then he explains the procedure and asks me if I'm okay with having it done. I'm not sure anyone has ever asked me for my opinion, and I'm quiet when he does.

"Whatever you think is best," I say. What I mean is, where I come from, it doesn't matter what I want.

While we wait for the surgery to be scheduled, I stay in Grandma's house again, behind the drawn curtains, kept closed day and night to shield Grandma from prying eyes while she grieves Grandpa, the ruler of our world. I suspect widows and windows are both immovable, because Grandma mostly stays in bed, and when I reach behind each curtain to check the window latches, twisting them to see if I can get the seal to break, they all remain put.

Grandma and I spend a lot of time in the dark together. Sometimes she plays Grandpa's devotions on her cassette player, as loud as the volume will go, and Grandpa's voice infiltrates the air we breathe.

When Becca calls me, she says they do this at the Field too, filling the pavilion with Grandpa's proclamations of impending terror. Becca says they all believe his prognostications for the end of the world, and they look like they're sitting there waiting for the *untimely figs* to appear on a fig tree, except no one we know has a fig tree, not even Aunt Bernice.

"Maybe it wouldn't be such a bad thing," I say, "for the trumpet to sound. Then we could run to the Mountain together and eat acorns and pine nuts and throw rocks at those who curse us."

Becca tells me she asked Mother if she could visit me, but Mother said no.

I sleep on the fold-out chair with Sois and Little One and Lady. I lick my skin, as if it is a wound I can clean. Grandma's house is only fifty yards from the activity at the Field, but we are on the outskirts of the hallowed land of the furrowed Field, and whatever life grows there does not cross over into the margins of our existence.

No one comes to visit Grandma, and no one comes to visit me.

I imagine myself as a leper, left to die outside of the compound. Grandma's backyard is all asphalt and concrete, but in the sliver of the side yard I can see from the one little window in her study, there is an old rosebush, which doesn't look like it's been tended to in years. I stare at that domesticated bush with longing, thinking of the Tehachapi rose hips we would eat on the Mountain, back when we were wild.

Away from the Mountain, I have forgotten what it feels like to walk on the earth. I have lost most of the feeling in my extremities, and I can't remember what it feels like to be home.

Now that Grandpa is gone, no one comes to the house to clean, so sometimes I go days without talking to anyone. I have read all of Grandma's magazines and everything in her file cabinet and dresser drawers, which is mostly just copies of Bible questionnaires and sheet music. I look out every window in the house except the ones in Mildred's room, because I still haven't managed a way to get in there. I'm hoping to see a change in the sky, waiting for the sun *to be turned into darkness, and the moon into blood, before the great and the terrible day of the Lord* is upon us.

I know this is just temporary, and being stuck in here is for my own protection, but that doesn't make it easier. Off prednisone my platelets are so low now they say I could bleed to death from a scratch.

If the operation works, I could go back to normal, though I'm not sure I know what that looks like. If it doesn't, I could have to stay here forever and I may turn out like Aunt Mildred.

Everything about being here makes me feel old. Aunt Mildred seems really old, like way older than Mother, even though she's Mother's younger sister, by a long shot. Maybe this is who I will be one day, emerging from my locked room to throw things or accuse Lizbeth's or Becca's daughters of trying to burn up the house with electric devices.

I watch Grandma in her long white nightgown kneel by her bed to pray out loud. She prays for all of our souls, and for the future of the Field, and for her husband's work to be honored and continue to flourish. She does not pray for me to get well.

I feel sad for her, and after she's asleep, sometimes I climb onto the bed and lie next to her as she snores. My body is still, and my breath is steady, though I feel burdened with a truth I can't yet speak, even to myself.

Grandpa made fun of Grandma for her weight and demanded she stay thin, so Grandma mostly keeps her refrigerator stocked with sugar-free Jell-O pudding cups, and cans of Tab. But sometimes she forgets his shaming and notices I am thin. Then she'll go to the store and come back with a bag of ingredients, and, seemingly without thinking, she'll make salmon cakes and pork chops, rolling the meat into an egg and bread-crumb mixture, frying it in sizzling oil on the stove. On Saturdays, sometimes she drives to Kentucky Fried Chicken, and brings back coleslaw and mashed potatoes, and gravy in little foam cups, and squishy golden biscuits.

Although most of the time Grandma doesn't seem to notice I live here, when she's at the kitchen table doing puzzles, she'll look up at me over the glasses she wears around her neck on a little pearl chain and ask if I want to place a piece. I look down at my white skin, and it looks older than Grandma's. Sometimes I pretend not to hear her, because I feel like a ghost.

I need to get well, and I need to get out of here.

When Mother picks me up to take me to my hospital appointments, she parks out front and honks. She never comes into the house, but she doesn't say why.

Maybe she doesn't want to see Aunt Mildred come out of her room, screaming at me for working for the government. Hearing about Mildred trying to get me out of her house is different from watching it happen. I've told Mother about Aunt Mildred many times, and about how Grandma seems confused and doesn't correct her anymore, and how Grandma is forgetting more things; sometimes she doesn't even know who I am.

My body itches like I'm shedding my skin.

Things have been changing at the Field since Grandpa's death, but I get to hear about them only when Mother picks me up, or when Becca calls Grandma's house and I lock myself in the bathroom with the phone. The older Eriksen brother has officially taken over leadership, which we all knew would happen, since he ran things whenever Grandpa was on the road. But his authority is mostly ceremonial. Some of the leaders who have been followers of Grandpa for decades are jockeying for the real power, which they try to make look like a competition for holiness.

They pray fervently and hold many meetings. Mother rises, because she is smart and competent. A woman can't be in charge of anything spiritual, but the Eriksens have been part of the family since before she was born. Whoever is the head, Mother will be the neck of, determining what he looks at, what he notices, where the Field will go next. She has decided there needs to be more education and a real school, which she will run. She will teach young people what they need to know.

When I am well, I will go to Mother's school, but for now, I see her only when she takes me to the hospital. I want to put my head in her lap as she drives, or reach for her hand in the waiting room, or hug her after my tests, like I see other children doing. Sometimes I move very slowly, slithering up to her when she's not paying attention. I watch the way other parents hold their children, how they give them affection with their bodies, and I try to sit closer to Mother, so that I can feel the touch of her leg next to mine. She notices and pushes me away and tells me that's not appropriate.

I don't know what's appropriate for humans. When it comes to humans, I know only the identifying characteristics of apex predators and how to appease them.

When I am admitted back into Children's Hospital for the blood transfusions and other preparations necessary before the splenectomy, I have a roommate named Gayle, who is thirteen, like me. On our first day together, we know enough about blood counts and needle marks, bone marrow tests, cafeteria menus, diet soft drinks, and jealous siblings to keep up a constant chatter and bond like comrades in arms. She has hosts of visitors, in and out all day, who bring her get-well gifts, and her side of the room is filled with flowers and balloons. Her people talk to me and they tell us we could be sisters, twins even. We keep our window shade open, grateful for our corner view of the mountains, and we keep our television off so we can talk.

Our wristbands dictate what can and can't be done to us, but I feel more free here in the hospital than I do at Grandma's house. Gayle and I aren't part of a school or a class or a circle of girls, and our conversations aren't bound by social expectations. We thrive on imagination and hypothesis. When no one is visiting, Gayle speaks of boys with love and longing, and I tell her someday a boy will love her. She says she wants a boy to love her enough to bring her flowers, to invite her into his world, to introduce her to his friends and family, to claim her as his own and take care of her until death.

I don't tell her no one has ever brought me flowers or candy, or any of the things she has on her side of the room, nor do I tell her the other truth of which I am certain—that it's never going to happen to either of us, because sick girls aren't the kind of girls that boys worship.

Instead, I tell her how much I hate my wayward hair, and how jealous I am that hers always looks so perfect. She says it's modeled to look like Farrah Fawcett. I don't know who that is, but I tell her that's how I want mine to look.

She laughs and takes off her wig and tosses it over to me. She tells me to try it on. I press all my hair tight against my head and slip it on like a hat. I'm sure I look ridiculous, but she claps and says I look just like Farrah.

This is the first time I have seen Gayle's bald head. She reminds me of Sandra, confident, courageous, vulnerable, and doomed.

I picture Sandra's father kneeling at her bedside, his trembling prayers supplicating our heavenly Father with the desperation of a dying man. Sandra's father didn't know that God is a jealous God, without mercy, *visiting the iniquity of the fathers upon the children unto the third and fourth generation.*

My own father doesn't tolerate crying for any reason, dying or not. If he were here, he would tell me to stop whining or he'll squish me like a stinkbug. He hasn't yet come to the hospital, but his voice is loud in my head, and I take it with me when they wheel me on my gurney into surgery, practicing respect, honor, integrity, and personal courage, like he taught me to do when going into battle.

I will always place the mission first. I will never accept defeat. I will never quit. I will never leave a fallen comrade.

A couple of weeks later, I am discharged with high hopes of a full recovery. Without a spleen, my platelets have come back to normal and my ITP is in remission.

Gayle and I hug goodbye and say our girlish good lucks, and I tuck her picture into my bag, her cursive writing on the back—*You have the best hair*—dotted with purple hearts, wide and smiling.

I return to the Mountain that spring, rife with the possibility of wellness. Our parents immediately take off for the summer. Now that Grandpa is dead, Mother will be accompanying Dad on the Trip with the boys, instead of us.

I stay back and write letters to Gayle with devoted regularity, thrilled to finally have an audience for my thoughts.

When Gayle stops writing to me seven weeks later, I am crushed, certain she has found a better girl to write to, someone who speaks her language better than I do. I feel sorry for myself, but by the time I turn fourteen, slithering around the Devil's Punchbowl like a snake seeking affection, I am determined to teach my rattle to sing in my hands.

Not long after that, I receive a short note from Gayle's parents, informing me that my friend has passed away.

I can't see any point in getting better or growing up. Life seems paper-thin and fragile; anything can rip it wide open. I secure Gayle's letters and her picture under my mattress and stop eating.

Lay not up for yourselves treasures upon earth, where moth and rust doth corrupt, and where thieves break through and steal: But lay up for yourselves treasures in heaven, where neither moth nor rust doth corrupt, and where thieves do not break through nor steal: For where your treasure is, there will your heart be also.

MOTHER'S SCHOOL REQUIRES all its students to learn piano and to spend time on the Mountain learning about the Lord and the land. Lizbeth and I are two of the nine girls at the Field who are between the ages of fourteen and nineteen. There are eighteen boys in this age range, and the twenty-seven of us become an official high school, with Mother as our principal. When the boys get back from the Trip, they come up from the Field on a bus, and Lizbeth and I move out of the house and join them, sleeping in outdoor A-frames, using the outhouse, and meeting in the mess hall every day to become unified in our group beliefs.

Uncle Stephen is in charge of teaching all of us about the Bible. He has spent the last few days preaching to us about the difference between the beliefs of the Pharisees and the Sadducees and making us answer questions about Judaic law.

We sit on wooden benches that look like pews, and he stands in front of us, gesticulating. We can tell that Uncle Stephen knows a lot about these two religious groups, but most of us can't understand the details, or what they have to do with us and the world we are living in. From what I gather, the Pharisees were concerned with serving the God they knew from the books of law, while the Sadducees, a more prominent and liberal sect, pursued political and economic gains. Uncle Stephen rails against politics and capitalism and the two-party system, and most of the students are bored by his rants, but I am transfixed.

The way he describes how the Pharisees use religion to make themselves righteous reminds me of everything we do at the Field. He says that Jesus was the Messiah, that his appointed time was fulfilled, that he came not to bring peace but a sword, and that since the world did not believe, he will come again. He says that the majority will perish, and that whoever is saved will flee, and that the great tribulation and the revolt will come in our generation, leading to desolation and redemption.

Uncle Stephen tells us that most of Jesus's disciples were Pharisees and that, two thousand years later, so are Grandpa's, although we don't call ourselves that.

"The Pharisees followed Mosaic law to the best of their abilities," Uncle Stephen explains, "but they went overboard, because they didn't understand the spirit of the laws they were promulgating."

I laugh, but no one else finds this funny.

"Jesus took significant issue with them, because in their observance of rules and regulations, they were prideful and lost sight of the heart of God," he says. He tells us that the Pharisees were legalistic, and so they needed to catch Jesus on a technicality.

Whether they believed this would require an armed and bloody insurrection depends on who you ask, he says. Most wanted to await the Messiah in peace, hoping they could avoid a violent war.

There is something rattling the mess hall door. We all look toward the back of the room, where the door is shaking. At first I think it's just the wind, but now it sounds like someone is pounding on it. I assume one of us is missing and has been locked out, to teach a lesson, so I'm nonchalant about the noise, until a man in a ski mask breaks in, pointing a gun at all of us. He yells for us to get down.

Most of us fall to our knees, or lie prostrate under the benches. I can't hear anything. I feel myself rising out of my body as the room becomes silent. Everything around me vortexes into a straight line, and I feel as calm as I've ever felt. Time slows down, and I stand up and start to walk toward the man with the gun, certain I can offer him some kindness that will change his mind about whatever ill he wishes us. But before I get there, one of the bigger boys has jumped him and has him pinned to the ground. And then there is loud noise and chaos, and girls are screaming, and I am pulled back into my body, back into the family group of teenagers preparing for the end of the world. The man pulls off his mask and pushes himself up and out the door, and we let him go, because we recognize him. He is one of Grandpa's boys.

Uncle Stephen tells us all to settle down and sit in our seats. Everyone obeys, but we're all still talking. Eventually, Uncle Stephen yells, "Silence!" and the room quiets down.

"Take out your notebooks," he says.

"This is a test," he says. "Write your name on a clean sheet of paper, and answer these questions."

We all pull out paper and pencil, assuming we're back to dissecting Judaic law.

"Number one: What color was the man's shirt?"

Blue, I think. *Definitely blue.*

"Number two: What color was his mask?"

Black.

"Number three: What words did he speak?"

"Get down."

"Number four: Did he have a weapon, and if so, what kind?"

A .22 long rifle.

Uncle Stephen collects the papers. He thumbs through them and makes notes with his pen. He tells us the correct answers are blue, black, "Get down," and a .22 long rifle.

He doesn't say whether anyone has gotten all the answers right. That's not the point of this exercise. He tells us the point is that eyewitnesses are unreliable and don't corroborate one another's stories. That's why the Pharisees had a difficult time pinning Jesus to a specific crime. And that's why the Sanhedrin couldn't come to a consensus, and why Pontius Pilate sent Jesus to King Herod to be tried, and why it was put upon the high priest Caiaphas to break Jewish law.

I'm willing to believe whatever Uncle Stephen is saying. But that's not what I take away from this lesson. Whatever he intended, I've learned I can trust what I see with my own eyes.

Violence is everywhere, and no one around here seems to care, least of all the God of my fathers. I don't know this yet, but trusting my own experience over the party line will be how I piece together an exit strategy.

After this lesson, we are sent out to private devotions, to reflect on what we have learned and commune with God in nature. Today I walk up past the upper campfire ring to the east, off trail, to a gigantic fallen log, surrounded by wild Tehachapi rose bushes. Before I climb up on the log, I take off my shoes.

God called unto him out of the midst of the bush, and said, Moses, Moses. And he said, Here am I. And he said, Draw not nigh hither: put off thy shoes from off thy feet, for the place whereon thou standest is holy ground.

The roses aren't in bloom. The roses died long ago, but they have left behind little dried rose hips all over the branches. I pluck one off and put it in my mouth, chewing it gently, tasting its bitterness before I swallow it like a pill.

I picture Gayle's flowers, how they surrounded her like Grandpa's coffin. I wonder what happened to her family. I look down at my body. For the first time in a very long time, I think I may grow up. I touch the curve of my hip, feeling the way it juts away from my navel, like the sandstone in the Devil's Punchbowl, pushing its way out of the waters.

The curving beauty of my changing body is too much to bear. Not only for the boys who might lust after it, but for me too.

I have stopped eating meals, and my periods have gone away, but it's not enough. I need to cut back more. Sometimes the hunger feels painful to my body, punishing, damaging, deteriorating my being. But I'm comfortable with damage. It feels like home.

David wanted Bathsheba's body and, as king, he commanded her presence. Bathsheba lost both her husband, Uriah, and her child because of David, who she probably thought loved her. It seems to me that what David really did was worship her beauty, and God punished him for coveting her, like worshipping a golden calf. Bathsheba's baby dies to punish David, and Uriah dies for his loyalty to David. And nobody, not even God, has pity on Bathsheba for being the vessel.

She should have hidden herself away from the eyes of men, because if you're not seen, you can't be hunted.

I fill my pockets with rose hips, in case I need something to tide me over later. I don't want to turn into a woman. At least the kind of woman who becomes a wife, which is the only kind of woman I know.

I won't eat the food the Field provides. I won't eat anything at all. I will never be satiated, like Lizbeth is, never be the kind of girl who does as she is told without questioning. I will never grow into the good woman Grandpa wanted me to be.

I watch my body go back in time, becoming a young girl again, and I am proud of my discipline.

I may be a bad girl, but that's far better than being a woman. In fact, a bad girl may be almost as good as being a boy.

Coulter Pine

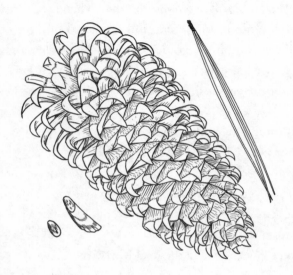

The Coulter pine, often called the big-cone pine, is native to the mountains of Southern California. It grows up to 85 feet tall, with a trunk of up 3 feet in diameter, and it has large yellow-brown cones, with hooklike projections that look like seagulls.

Coulter pines thrive in a wide variety of soils and can live over 100 years. Saplings can grow in partial shade, as long as the soil doesn't dry out. Mature Coulter pines can live without much water and can survive in shade or sun.

The trees have upturned branches, with 6- to 12-inch-long gray-green needles that grow in bundles of three. They produce the largest and heaviest cones of any known pine *species, which stay on the tree for 3 to 4 years and weigh up to 11 pounds each. Known colloquially as "widow-makers," these giant pine cones are often covered in a thick, sticky resin.*

Each cone carries about 150 seeds, which are sealed in tight with resin and will usually stay there until a fire melts the resin, drying out the cone, after which the cone opens and reveals its seeds. You can pry out these big, nutritious, oil-rich seeds with a thin stick, or you can put them in a fire pit to help them open. If you have the time to harvest them, you can eat the seeds, raw or cooked, for needed calories, while enjoying their delicious vanilla flavor.

THE FIELD'S INTERCOM IS LOUD, and no matter whose voice is on the speaker, it carries easily across the property, so I always know who's on CQ, in charge of the quarters. Today, Thomas's voice calls for Michelle and Danny to report to the office. Where we come from, there is no need for last names.

Thomas tells my brother and me that a storm is coming and that we need to get home to the Mountain early today. He says our parents are waiting for us in the truck.

We head to the back forty, where Dad works on vehicles and where he nearly always parks his Mazda truck. It's empty, but we climb in and wait.

I don't know where Becca is, but it looks like it's only me and Danny today. Lizbeth doesn't come up to the Mountain much anymore. She wants to be close to the Field, and Grandma likes having someone responsible there, with Mildred getting more out of control.

When our parents arrive, they don't speak to us, and I think that's my fault. Before Dad starts the truck engine, I can usually hear what our parents say to each other, and today, there is something off, so I shush Danny and pay close attention. But they aren't talking to each other right now. Mother sits in the front seat and starts reading her book on the taxonomy of birds, looking at a picture and covering the words with her hands, mumbling each kingdom, phylum, subphylum, class, order, family, genus, and species from memory. Her voice is so soft I can't tell if she's getting them right.

Dad gets in and starts the engine without saying a word, and we jolt forward, more abruptly than usual. Mother pauses her mumbling and looks over at him. As we drive up out of the basin of the Field, the sound of the engine gets louder, and I watch her head turn toward him so forcefully I can see her lips, which seem to be saying, "Dear, please."

Dad drives faster than I'm used to, and Danny and I bounce around in the back of the truck. We are annoyed at first, but then we start to laugh. Danny says he needs to pee, and I look around for an empty soda bottle, so that he won't get us both wet.

I settle into the corner and brace myself with my feet. I ask Danny if he remembers Grandpa's cliff story, the one he used to tell about how to hire a driver for your horse and buggy. Danny shrugs, as if he's heard too many stories to keep them straight.

I don't know anyone with a horse and buggy, but Grandpa had so much enthusiasm when he would tell this story—with the inflections in his voice, how he stressed the action, the way he paused before the punch line, looking at us intently, like he was teaching us something important—that I would always listen. It felt important to listen, to let myself live in a world of horses and buggies so I could feel the power of his gaze.

"Tell me," Danny says.

So I begin. "There once was a wealthy man who needed goods delivered to a faraway town. He was too busy to take them himself, so he set out to hire a driver." I squint my eyes and look around, like Grandpa used to, as if searching for an appropriate candidate. "He narrows his choices down to three men, who he will take up a mountain," I continue, raising my fingers slowly, to add to the drama. "'Show me your driving skills on this road,' the rich man says, giving each of them the reins of his prized steed. The first man carefully steers the cart toward the cliff and expertly rides along the edge."

I lift my arms and imitate holding reins, showing the motions of a driver trotting along in a cart. Danny laughs, so I become more dramatic, pulling my whole body back sharply, the way Grandpa used to, veering side to side as I continue imitating the man.

Grandpa used to tell this story as if it were fresh every time. He must have forgotten we had heard this story before, in club meetings, chapel, and church, so that we already knew every word by heart.

"Then ever so skillfully, the man pulls the horses back, showing the owner his command of the buggy," I tell Danny. "This annoys the second man, who says, 'That's nothing. Watch this!' And he steers the horses even closer to the edge of the cliff, so close that their hooves push the loose gravel down the hill. Then he triumphantly pulls them away to safety.

"The third man takes the reins without a word and calmly drives the horses around the turn as close to the mountain as he can, avoiding the cliff by a good ten feet.

"The rich man is clearly pleased with this last man's choices, and he makes his proclamation. 'It is clear that you all know how to drive. But I value prudence over skill. You, sir,' he says to the third driver, 'you are the man for the job.'"

Grandpa always folded his arms when he finished this story, so I do this too, nodding at Danny with the condescension of authority.

Even though I know the tale was meant to teach us a moral lesson, not serve as the vehicle for the sensuous sensations of danger buzzing around in my head, I feel excited, just thinking about the edge. Grandpa said if we took chances in life, we would fall headlong from a cliff, plunging to our deaths on the rocks below.

But still, I want to be the driver who drives as close to the edge as possible.

The storm we're expecting hasn't arrived, but we still have a long hike in, because the snow has been building up for weeks. I wish we had the snowmobile Dad recently borrowed from Ski Sunrise, across the way. He said we would use it to pack in our things, but it's up in the garage, not down here near the road, where it could actually be useful. I don't know how he convinced the people at the ski area that it was in their best interest to let us keep one of their machines for the

winter, but I know he didn't pay them. Dad is gifted at the art
of seduction, like Grandpa was, making people feel compelled
to offer him something valuable with no compensation.

I'm often ashamed of being the recipient of charity, but
when it comes to a snowmobile, it doesn't feel like weakness.
Dad says the best way to learn is by watching, so I've watched
every step of what he does to make that thing run. He hasn't
let me drive it alone yet, but he's taught me the basics and
even lets me start the engine before he hurls away, the snow
rising up like smoke, leaving no tracks except billowing powder puffs and the illusion of magic.

After I peel off my wet things, I go to find Becca. She's in
her room, pushing Matchbox cars around the carpet while
making a sound a little like an engine but more like a dying
animal.

I know something is wrong. Not from her words, because
she says nothing. Not even from her bruised face, because we
are not fragile and bruises don't derail us. I know from the
way her breath is making a noise in her throat that's not in
sync with the sound of the cars.

"Tell me what happened," I say.

Becca shrugs, like it's no big deal.

I wait, because after being sick for years, I have lots of
experience with waiting.

"Dad lost his temper," she says.

I don't hug her, even though I want to. I'm afraid she'll
crumble from the weight of my touch.

"How bad?"

"Bad," she says, moving the little car around like she's

a young child, but she doesn't cry. She, too, has learned the lesson Mother has taught.

I get close enough to touch Becca's hair, which is short, like a boy's. But she doesn't look like a boy. She is as tall as I am, and her breasts are bigger than mine, probably because I don't eat anymore. I reach out to stroke her head, but she pulls away from my hand, hunching in her chin toward her collarbone. She keeps pushing around the cars on the floor, making those noises that make me uncomfortable.

I climb up onto her bed and get under the covers.

"How could you do this to me?" she says.

"Do what?" I ask.

"That's what he kept saying, over and over: 'How could you do this to me?'"

I want to get up and get closer to her, but Mother believes touch is for children, and coddling is for babies. Becca has her period now, and she is practically a woman, so she can't possibly need touch anymore.

"He kept asking me why, and he kept hitting me, telling me to apologize. I couldn't apologize. I didn't do anything wrong."

"What did you do?"

She shakes her head. "I just feel sorry for him."

"Feel sorry for Dad?"

"He was just so out of control, like he wanted to control me, but he couldn't control himself. He wanted me to say I was sorry, or cry, or be ashamed. But I'm not."

I peek my head out. She's not playing with the cars, but she's not looking at me either.

"He kept hitting me because I wouldn't say I was sorry. I think it scared him, how hard he was hitting, but he just kept telling me to wipe the smirk off my face."

"What did you do?"

She climbs in next to me, and I wrap my body around her, spooning her, so she still doesn't have to look at me. It's been years since we've been close like this, but it feels natural, like we're puppies.

"I just want to be a boy," she says. "I want to play Snake in the Grass or Kick the Can and have rubber-band gun wars."

"Where was Mother?" I ask.

"She stood there quiet, with that stern look of hers."

"What made Dad so angry?"

"I kissed Jose."

"On purpose?" I ask, surprised this was possible.

Grandpa's story makes a different kind of sense to me now. What if driving too near the edge is like kissing a boy, and having sex before marriage with someone who can get you pregnant is like falling headlong from a cliff, plunging to your death on the rocks below.

Do they just want us to be safe?

When I look at Becca from this angle, she looks small, like Danny, like the little sister she used to be. I wouldn't want Grandpa's boys to have sex with her.

"He didn't make you?" I say, and Becca shakes her head no.

I don't know what I'm feeling, but I want to keep holding Becca close now and I want to protect her from whatever comes next. Maybe that's why we're not allowed to stay together at the same Field houses. Maybe that's why we're not allowed to call each other or acknowledge our sisterhood. Maybe this protective feeling is the kind of attachment that's a sin.

Maybe our parents' fear is about bonding. Maybe choosing one person over another or wanting to be around one person more than another is dangerous to the unity of the group. Maybe our sisterhood is dangerous because if we protect each other, we'll stop doing what they say.

I feel trapped in this room, thick with the weight of the things we're not saying. I'm cold and wet and tired, and I don't want to be here, but I can't walk out. I don't trust God to protect Becca, and if that makes me a sinner, then I'm a sinner. Someday I will leave, and when I figure out where there is to go, I will come back for Becca and take her there too.

I take off my sweatshirt and look at my tiny white arms. The blue veins show through all along the insides of my forearms. They look like rivers. I run my fingers along the needle marks on the insides of my elbow creases and on the inner edges of the papery skin on my wrists, and I want to protect Becca from this, from the pain of tenderness.

Mother speaks publicly from a pulpit about David, the man after God's own heart, who was summoned from the field where he was tending the flock so he could be anointed king of Israel.

But Mother raised us to be sheep.

Unlike the shepherd David, who defeated the giant Goliath and then sinned against God by getting Uriah's wife, Bathsheba, pregnant, we aren't the chosen ones. David had Uriah killed, and then when David's advisor Nathan reprimanded him, he repented and was forgiven and went on to have more babies with Bathsheba, one of whom grew up to be King Solomon, whose words are my favorite in the whole Bible.

Is that redemption or just being a man? I can't think of any girls in the Bible who are afforded such grace.

Becca's breath begins to slow, and I can feel her body soften.

Later, Mother will tell me that God asked her to sacrifice her blood children, like Abraham set out to do with Isaac, when he tied him to an altar, raising his knife to strike him dead. She says this is how God tests our faith, by taking away what we love. But the only thing I care about tonight is all the ways she taught us it's dangerous to attach.

I believe either of our parents would kill us if God asks them to.

If I had a sling, like David used in his fight with Goliath, I would use it to fight Dad. But I don't have a sling, so I stay curled up next to Becca all night, listening to her breathe. I wish I were a sheepdog.

In the morning, I climb out of her bed and look out the window, watching the snow turn pink with the glow of the sun as it rises across the morning sky. The snow covers everything, so that you can't see any of the dirt or rocks or pine needles that lie underneath.

It looks like the entire mountain has been washed in the blood of the Lamb and come out pure. I want the serenity of that snow more than I have ever wanted anything.

Becca's breath is still warm and even, and I tiptoe out to the sound of her sleep. I go to the garage and find the keys at the bottom of the toolbox where I saw Dad hide them. I finger the ragged edges like a first kill, then slide them into my bra and look for a coat and boots. Once dressed, I drag the snowmobile out onto the meadow behind the house, the keys cold against my breasts.

I've been taught I'm a vessel to be used, and now that I am fifteen, it may be too late to see myself any other way. But if I don't find a way to come back for Becca, she may die in this place and it will be my fault.

I pull the cord several times, revving the engine. I climb on, and the motor vibrates through the seat of the vehicle and up into my hips. I release the brake and head down the ravine and over the campfire ring buried beneath the snow, maneuvering in and out of the trees, gaining momentum.

If I'm not seen, I can't be hunted.

I ride farther and farther from the boundary of our camp, but I stay within the path of the trees, relying on them for protection.

Freedom is the distance between a predator and its prey, and while I am riding on this thing, I am as far away as I have ever been from the Field's rules and as close as I've ever been to freedom.

Something massive rains down from the sky, and I swerve to avoid it. It kerplunks deep into the snow. I want to keep going, ignoring it, pretending I am both wild and free, but I am too curious and there is too much at stake. Maybe this is a sign.

I stop the engine and walk back to the crater in the snow.

I reach into the hole and pull out a Coulter pine cone, as heavy as a baby. I pick it up and hold it tenderly, like it's a gift from heaven. Although it's late in the season, I run my cold fingers along the edges of the cone, looking for an entry point to extract a seed. The scales look like carving, like the woodwork on our altar at the Field.

I feel a sharp pain on one of my fingers, and I jump, like I've been bitten. I drop the cone, heeding its warning, and shove my finger in my mouth. I suck on it for comfort from the insult of the attack. I can see a slice across the tender skin of my middle finger, where one of the talons wedged into my skin, drawing blood. It's a clean wound, and it was my fault for trying to pull out a seed. I should have remembered the cones are locked tight until next autumn.

I leave the cone buried in the snow, trusting it to protect itself through the winter. I get back on the snowmobile and turn on the motor, filling the forest with the sound of fury.

I am a starving girl, thin and hungry in the morning air, but I will ride this thing until I run out of gas, because I would rather be bad than powerless.

I don't care if the Apocalypse comes now or never. This swiftness is mine. This vengeance is mine. So saith the Lord.

Chokecherry

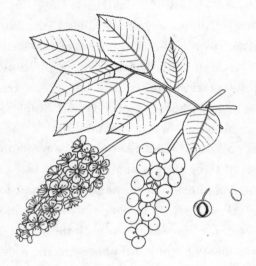

The chokecherry grows mostly in heavily wooded thickets, either on small trees or on shrubs, in damp places up to 8,200 feet elevation. In the spring, the plant has clusters of white flowers, and in the summer and fall it produces small dark-crimson cherries.

You can eat chokecherries raw, but they are extremely tart. The leaves and the seeds contain cyanide, so be mindful to remove the pit if you eat the cherry raw.

Birds love the fruit so much they have scattered its seeds widely, making the chokecherry one of the most widely distributed trees in North America.

MOTHER SAYS TO BECOME GOOD women and wives, we must learn how to move in the world of men. This requires two things: always have something interesting to talk about, and always let a man think he is smarter than you.

I am good at both of those things, but there is nothing that feels useful to me about becoming a woman except the ability to make money. Now that I am fifteen, I have found a new way to collect cash without resorting to charity or donations meant for the Field. People wanting what I can contribute is satisfying. Being competent feels better than being fragile.

The Eriksens live on the border of the back forty. They have more money than we do, because Mr. Eriksen comes from a family that invested in homes back in the 1940s and '50s, and in Southern California, that means something. I don't know why he doesn't give all the money to the Field, like he's supposed to, but maybe his family protected it somehow. All I know is that he has enough money to buy his two daughters all sorts of things Lizbeth, Becca, and I wish we had, like tennis shoes, jeans, haircuts, and food. His daughter Tammy also has a bike, although I don't think she rides it, because none of us have anywhere to go.

Or at least anywhere we're allowed to go. I'm careful when I ask Tammy if I can borrow her bike. I tell her it's to run errands for my dad.

She shrugs, uninterested. "Yeah, sure," she says.

I offer to pay her, in the form of an IOU. She looks at me like I've lost my mind. "We're family," she says. "And anyway, you're never going to have money."

I say thank you, and I wish I could tell her how much this means to me, but no one I know talks about feelings, so I just ride away.

Through word of mouth, I build a housecleaning clientele. For some jobs, I go once a week. Others I do every other week or once a month. I keep a list in my journal that tells me when I should be where.

For some jobs, the house is empty. In addition to any regular duties, the woman in charge leaves a list of anything extra she needs done. These are the jobs I like best, because I have space to think while I work.

I use Tammy's bike to ride to these jobs, and my legs become strong from the miles I cover from one appointment to another.

Some of the women leave snacks out for me, or even access to a shelf in the refrigerator. Most of them appreciate me, because I make their lives easier, talking to their children or caring for them when they need to make phone calls or run errands. In one house, one of the husbands has shown me how to use the stereo, and when the empty house fills with his music, I work along to secular sounds and beats and words I have never heard before.

Occasionally, husbands are present at the initial intake interview, and they appreciate that I ask them questions about the various cleaning apparatuses, as well as the way I smile and nod and say thank you when they teach me things I already know. I watch each of their rhythms and respond to their needs, becoming whomever they need me to be.

Who knew Mother's training could be so useful?

I like being a house cleaner, because I like earning money, but also because I'm trusted inside these people's worlds, free to look at their things, free to move around in their closeted spaces, managing tangible things that can be tidied up. There aren't any precarious rules inside these houses. I organize and categorize concrete items, with lists the women give me, telling me what to prioritize. I study these lists. I learn what they value. I try to make sense of the exchange we are making, the money they give me for saving them time, how much it's worth to do menial tasks, what I can do to be worth more.

Money is how I will leave someday, how I won't get trapped like the other girls, how I won't have to get married and have babies and take my husband's name. I don't want to be a woman in the world as I know it. I don't want my breasts to grow in large and pendulous, like all the women in my family. I don't want hips to carry children. I don't want to be a vessel for a man's seed.

Boys at the Field don't have to get married. Some of them, like the oldest Mr. Eriksen, who is in charge of the circus, and Mr. Turner, who runs the head office, were in Grandpa's first troop in 1931 and have been single their whole lives.

There aren't enough girls at the Field for all of Grandpa's boys in their twenties and thirties, so the boys get to live single for as many years as it takes for a girl to become available. I listen to the boys who live with us when they talk about this. They have made a list of eligible girls, and while I'm on their list, I'm too old for most of them. Some of the boys in their late twenties and even thirties are waiting for girls younger than Becca to come of age, girls who haven't even gotten their periods yet.

Sometimes I stay alone in my grandmother's house while she goes on a missionary trip. Grandma hasn't given my sisters or me a key to her house, because Grandpa told her if she gave us a key, we would lose it and someone else would find it and come in and rape, murder, and dismember her. He has been dead for almost three years, but I guess she's not taking any chances. She has automatic locks, an alarm system, and various homemade booby traps, but I know how to use the dog door to get in. When Grandma is at home, whether Mildred is there or not, since she refuses to answer my knocking, I climb in and out of the dog door without Grandma noticing, sleeping or tossing fitfully on her couch, then riding Tammy's bike to as many jobs as I can squeeze in.

It's easier to earn money than it is to keep it, because Dad thinks the money belongs to him. He's taken all the money I've hidden under mattresses, even under the mattresses of my siblings. He doesn't make excuses for this. He just says the Lord provides in mysterious ways.

I don't have a bed or a drawer at Grandma's house, so I mostly hide money in cups on shelves too high for her to reach.

I never buy food with the money, of course, because I don't need food. If I have to eat something, I eat what's given to me at my jobs, or what Grandma won't notice I take.

Not eating much was hard at first, but now the dizzy rapture of starving makes me feel light, like I'm not subject to gravity, like I don't need the earth or any of its resources. I'm convinced I don't need the kinds of things other people do, so not having them doesn't bother me very much. I try not to subject myself to disappointment.

Sometimes I practice comfort control by denying what's offered to me by the households in which I work, because I don't want to get attached. I bite my nails, chew my hair, lose more weight. If I get smaller, I can't have a baby. If I get smaller, no one will notice me. If I get smaller, I can disappear, and no one will realize I have left.

I haven't had a period in four months. I feel untethered, unmoored. My dreams are filled with flying.

It's convenient not to bleed anymore, but sometimes I'm worried I could be pregnant. Grandpa's boys stopped touching me years ago, when I got sick, but I am worried anyway. What if one of his boys slept in my camp bed, committed onanism, and then when I came home, his sperm swam up inside me?

I ask Mother how hard it is for girls to get pregnant before they are married.

"That's not an appropriate discussion for a girl your age, and I won't have it in my house, do you hear me?"

Her anger reaches at me like a slap, and I step back.

Then she seems to soften, and she looks at me. "You wouldn't disappoint your father and me like that," she says.

I'm always disappointing someone. I don't know how to stop being a disappointment. Schooled in self-effacement, I want only to keep myself from wanting. I tell myself again that I will have no needs, not for clothes, food, touch, or people.

Not needing anyone or anything is the closest I can get to freedom.

Until one of Grandpa's boys calls out to me as I ride up the street to my job, asking me to wait. I stop, thinking I've been caught, that this is some sort of arrest.

"Here," the tall boy says, handing me a Snickers bar. "You might need backup today."

I take the candy, but I don't eat it. I ride away, and when I'm out of sight, I put it in my bra, where it stays all day, melting and forming a lump next to my heart.

The tall boy calls to me again the next day, but this time I don't stop.

He calls to me the day after that as well, but I am swift on Tammy's wheels and I get away. I don't want candy. I don't want anything except to acquire the money I will need to leave someday.

The next day, the tall boy tosses me something as I ride by. I catch it, the way Dad taught me to.

When I am out of sight, I look down to see what's in my hands. He has taped a note to a bag of gummy bears, as heavy as a heart. I'm not allowed to read notes from boys, but I read his.

He's known me for years, but he's careful not to write our real names, so we have plausible deniability, should anyone find our correspondence. He addresses me as Star, because he says I am always so far away, and because I will go places he will never go. He calls himself Teddy, because he says he will always be here to comfort me. I save his note and will hide it later, in one of Grandma's cups with my money. I feel safe knowing that if anyone finds it, they won't know who it's from.

The tall boy and I don't speak to each other, but he begins to leave candy and notes for me under the mat on Grandma's porch at night. I read the notes and eat the candy and write him back, leaving letters out in exchange for his.

Weeks turn into months, and I wait for his intermittent letters with the kind of hunger and longing I once had in the hospital, while hoping my family would come to visit.

I turn sixteen, riding long distances, subsisting on nothing but candy, writing letters to a teddy bear who speaks only in silence, his block-letter words, in pencil on notebook paper, echoing in my own voice inside my head.

As the autumn arrives, I begin to shiver. I am so cold I layer myself in Grandma's clothes, which hang off me like blankets. I layer myself in every item of clothing I can get my hands on, but I can't stop shivering.

When I shiver during worship, my teeth start rattling so loudly I think other people can hear them. People turn around and look over and stare, as if I'm having visions from the Lord.

I feel a flash of heat, like I've been struck by holiness, and when I stand up to go find water, the world turns black.

When I come to, the chairs are empty, and Mrs. Washington is there. She asks me if I know where I am.

"Is this heaven?" I ask.

She lifts my head and offers me a sip of orange juice from a carton. I shake my head no.

"Just water," I say.

"You need nutrients," she says, and holds the carton firmly to my lips. I take a sip.

She says I am running a fever and that Mr. Washington will carry me. He picks me up, and she walks with us. My head is slung over his shoulder, and I watch the ground rise and fall with his steps. I hope I'm not too heavy. I hope I'm not hurting him. He puts me in the back seat of their car, and I lie down.

They say my parents will be coming soon.

The Washingtons drive me down to Los Angeles, back to the same hospital I left three years ago. When Dr. Shore does his rounds in the morning, he says that my parents are snowed in but that the nurses will take good care of me until they arrive.

He doesn't tell me how many days it will be before they arrive, and I don't know if he meant to say *they*. Dad has never stepped foot in this hospital. I don't know why he would come now.

Dr. Shore says I have pneumonia and I am dangerously thin. He tells me my IV has antibiotics and nutrients and that if I want to leave the hospital, I need to listen to what he says. He tells me I need to eat and that I must demonstrate I can eat before they let me go.

My parents don't come to visit, but, in time, the tall boy does.

The tall boy's mom pokes her head into the hospital room doorway to say, "Hey there, sweet face," and then asks me how I'm feeling and tells us she will be in the waiting room until her son has finished his visit.

He sits down in the chair next to my bed, on the opposite side of my IV pole. It is the first time we've ever seen each other at eye level. He reaches for my left hand, where the needle is taped in on top, touching my fingers gently, then carefully inserting his own into the webbing of mine.

He is breaking the Field's rules to be here, and so is his mom, but she is an Outsider, and not subject to the ritual of excommunication, nor the threat of it.

He sits with me, his hand linked in mine, for an hour without talking. No one has ever held my hand before.

I close my eyes and pull in the emotion like a syringe, softening my face so that the tears won't emerge. My mother has taught me well. I look at the tall boy's face—he has a chipped tooth—and I look at his fingers, carefully curled around the needle taped onto my hand, and I don't cry or ask for anything.

"Luke," I say. I feel safe to use his real name here, and I like it.

He doesn't smile, and he doesn't promise me anything, and I don't even know how long he stays because I fall asleep to the sound of his breath. In the morning, I find a candy bar and a note on my hospital tray.

When I get back to the Mountain, Lizbeth has taken over the role of director for the Easter sunrise service passion play. I am accustomed to playing Mary Magdalene, but she says I haven't been cast this year.

"What about one of the other women at the tomb?" I ask. "Am I playing one of the other women?"

"You're not in the play," she says, "because if Jesus arose, you're not the kind of girl he would talk to. And you're not the kind of girl he'd come back to either."

I think that's a mean thing to say, but if Luke or his mom told anyone they came to the hospital, she might have heard about it and that would give her the right to weigh my actions on the scales of justice and find me wanting.

I stand still and watch her writing in her notebook. I think I could write a better play than she can, but I don't say that. I don't say anything at all.

"You made your choice," she adds, and she turns away from me.

Lizbeth is right. I'm not the kind of girl who would wait at Jesus's tomb for an appearance that may or may not happen. I'm not the kind of girl who waits patiently for the end of the world or the kind of girl who will be called to rise when the trumpet sounds. And I'm definitely not the kind of girl anyone will come back for. I'm the kind of girl who people leave alone in hospitals, and for the next two decades, I will believe that makes me unlovable.

For now, I bow to her judgment; I don't deserve to be a woman at the tomb.

When the snow begins to thaw, I want to explore the earth as I know it, so I write a note inviting Luke to the Mountain.

I climb out my bedroom window and arrive at our designated meeting place early, tucking myself into the hollow of a black oak, feeling more intimacy with the Mountain in the darkness than I do in the light. I think about what the Bible means when it talks about darkness and night and the earth as the devil's domain, as if what exists in the shadows is something to avoid.

Yea, though I walk through the valley of the shadow of death, I will fear no evil: for thou art with me.

Luke said he would borrow his mom's car and park at the ranger station, that he would hike up the dirt road to the mess hall, and meet me here at midnight.

It's 11:57 when I see him approach, the bright blue of his jacket reflecting the moon. He looks around nervously when the coyotes howl. I don't call out to calm him. I just watch and listen.

When he's within a few yards of me, I stand up. "Follow me," I say. "I'll show you my home."

Luke jumps when he hears my voice. He's been to the Mountain with a group, but he's never explored it on his own, doesn't know any part of it that's not on a designated trail. We haven't walked more than fifty feet when he trips on a rock and lands on his knees. I scramble to help him, and he pushes me away.

I pick pebbles from the indentations on my feet while he tends to his pride.

"You're barefoot," he says. "That's against the rules."

"Easier to feel my way around in the dark."

I spread my toes and brush off the dirt in the webbing between them. My feet love the earth, like my hair loves the wind. We hike all the way to the top road in silence, and then I turn him around and we look at the moon.

I think a lot about rules these days. Tamar, Rahab, Ruth, and Bathsheba. The women who get credit for producing Jesus didn't follow rules. Men were in charge of their lives, and they maneuvered in whatever ways they needed to survive. Did Grandma think about that when she taught me their stories?

I pick yerba santa for Luke to chew on, so he won't be thirsty on our way back.

"Are you sure that's safe?" he says.

"I'm sure," I say. "Holy weed is a medicine. It's even listed in the 1894 *US Pharmacopoeia* as an official remedy for coughs, pneumonia, and bronchitis."

"How do you know that?" he asks.

"I know a lot of things that aren't particularly useful."

I know it's a sin to talk and laugh and hike this moonlit mountain, but we do it anyway, and I show him how to eat what the earth provides. I point out the chokecherries, hidden among the willows that grow at the bend in the road, and I tell him I will make chokecherry jam for him the next time he comes up. He says he would like that.

WHEN WE ARE AT THE FIELD, he pretends he doesn't know me. The only way I can see him when I'm staying down in the valley is if I wait for him in the trunk of his mom's car, which she lets him use, since she's not a leader and doesn't care what the rules are down here in the basin of the Field. He doesn't lock his car, because we are a safe community. No one locks anything at the Field. We don't have locks—not for our bikes or on doors, not even in bathrooms.

When he approaches, he knocks and I kick my foot up hard against the trunk's interior so he knows I'm there. I stay in there while he drives us up somewhere in the suburban hills, away from the eyes of the followers.

I feel like maybe I'm the kind of girl Grandpa talked about, who deserves to be put into a trunk and chopped up into pieces and mailed home to her parents, but I don't want Luke to think that's the kind of girl I am, so I set some parameters.

"Here are the rules," I tell him, crawling out of his trunk and putting my hands on my jutting hip bones. "We can't hold hands or kiss. If you want to spend time with me, you have to promise not to touch me."

He laughs, certain I am joking, which gets me defensive.

"I may not be the kind of girl who will get into heaven," I say, "but while I'm living on this earth, I'm not going to have a baby."

He asks me if I'm ever scared.

"Scared of what?" I counter. There's nothing to be scared of in the hills. As long as we're outside and away from people and their rules, I know how to find everything we need.

As the summer rolls in, I sleep next to my window, which I leave open to feel the air. One night, there is a cold hand on my thigh, but I don't jump. I reach out and put my hand in his, knowing instinctively whose it is, even though I am half-asleep. He has awkwardly climbed through my window and settled himself on top of me. I turn my head, because if I let him kiss me, I will go to hell.

He lies on top of me, and I feel his erection driving into my hip. He begins to hyperventilate. I ask him what is wrong, if he's ill? He says it is the altitude, and I believe him.

He starts to remove my covers, to come in closer, and I tell him to stop, that touching me is a sin. Underneath my friendly red blanket, I am wearing a T-shirt and gym shorts and nothing else.

But it's a warm night, so I take his hand and pull him out of my window, holding on tight as we hike up the road together in the moonlight. I put my free hand on my lips, signaling to him not to speak.

He holds my hand and kisses me on the cheek, and nestles his nose along my neck until he finds my lips, where he stays, and I let him.

I no longer feel the ground beneath me.

I am sixteen years old and have broken my covenant with God. I have kissed a boy and will no longer be pure at the altar of my marriage. I'm probably ruined for marriage altogether, but that doesn't bother me as much as knowing I'm inherently unlovable, and that Luke will eventually figure that out and leave me. I have swallowed Mother's words like knives, and whenever I feel love, I will bolt, as if darting from a predator, as if running to survive.

I tell him he can't come up here anymore. I tell him we're through.

I run down the hill barefoot, and I don't look back.

WHEN IT'S TIME for the next Trip, Luke gets on the bus with my father. I stand alone on the bank and watch them go. I don't wave, though I have the right to, since Dad is driving the bus. I can't see Luke, but I know he is in there, surrounded by a throng of boys, who for the next ten weeks will keep him safe from the temptations of girls like me.

As they turn the corner and are out of sight, my abdomen convulses. I feel a sharp pain in my lower belly, and a well of warm liquid spills from between my thighs. I press my legs together and hold my breath. I wonder if I have wet my pants. It isn't until I look down and see the blood on the insides of my knees that I begin to sob. I don't want to be a woman. I don't want to stay back and bleed while the boys traverse the country, jumping in rivers.

I am supposed to attend the departure prayer meeting, but I can't go now.

I move quietly across the top of the bank, trying not to attract attention as I walk the fifty yards to Grandma's back gate, dripping blood like a wounded soldier. I disconnect the wire in the front security box and climb the fence that blocks her driveway. Lady is barking, but I pat her head before I hop down the last scale of the fence, and she backs off.

She bit me the first two times I tried this, but I have been feeding her snacks lately, so she likes me better now. Only a fool tries to change a creature's instincts. I flip the breaker that controls the alarm and squeeze through the dog door. It is a tight fit, but manageable. I hope I will be able to get this mess cleaned up before Grandma gets home and calls for backup, certain a murderer is lodging there.

I roll toilet paper around and around the crotch of my underwear to create some padding. I've read enough magazines and cleaned enough houses to know there are sanitary items made for this sort of thing, but I don't have any, and there's always something on hand I can use to make do.

I fall asleep on the couch. I dream I am at the Field and I am hungry. It is lunchtime, and I am upstairs in what was once Grandpa's office but is now a room set aside exclusively for prayer.

I am looking out the large one-way window at the field below, and the clouds grow dark. Lightning flashes, and it begins to rain, great big drops of dark water, turning into a torrential downpour, loud and heavy, pounding like hail against the tin roof. The lights flicker and shut down, and I am kneeling alone in the darkness. I think Grandpa's spirit must be alive in this room, and I am frantic with fear. I know that whatever he is doing in the other world, he does not wish me well. I flap my hands across the wall, feeling around for the doorknob. The door swings open, yanked by the wind, and I am outside, assailed by the torrent. My skirt flies up, and I struggle to hold it down while I hang on to the rail. I don't want to plummet into the rising water below.

I see Luke in the distance, holding an umbrella over his head. Only his shoes appear to be wet. I want to call out to him to come rescue me, but I don't think he will hear me in this downpour, and I'm afraid he will be submerged if he tries to come back for me.

The water is rising. I continue down the stairs until I am two steps from the bottom. If I go any farther, I will be knee-deep in water. The rain is coming down so fast I don't think I can make it to the street. I will be submerged before I get there. I wonder if I have the strength to swim against the current.

Lizbeth and Becca are in the leadership room, and they are gesturing to me to come join them. "Michelle, Michelle!" they say. "Come in here. Come out of the rain. You're getting soaked!" I look at them, but with the water streaming down my face, they look blurry.

I consider going to them. They look so safe and dry and cozy huddled in that room together, but I'm scared to cross the aqueous chasm. I look up the hill, and Luke is gone.

Lizbeth calls to me, "This is the only room open. It's the only dry place you'll find."

I'm just a girl, but I know better. I know that can't be the only safe place in the world.

"You'll drown!" Lizbeth screams. "If you stay there, it'll be too late!"

But I don't care. I don't care if I die in this rain. I don't care if they take everything away from me, if my life ends in this raging storm of vengeance. I will not enter.

I wake up when I hear Grandma come in. She doesn't ask any questions about how I got in or why I'm sleeping on her couch. She just sits down next to me and puts her hand on my knee. That's how I know something is wrong.

"My sister has passed."

I don't know what to say. Aunt Bernice was the love of Grandma's life. Maybe mine too.

"It's all right," she says finally, patting my knee. "She's with Grandpa now."

Lord have mercy.

I go with Grandma to a small funeral service in a church, surrounded by Friends. It's not their meetinghouse, but they're all here. When we get out of the car, Grandma pats my head and says, "Be good."

We sit in silence for the first ten minutes.

In the silence of the room, I listen to the still-soft voices inside my head. My mouth is moving before I realize I am speaking. Next to the coffin of Aunt Bernice, scripture breaks forth from my mouth.

"And Jacob was left alone; and there wrestled a man with him until the breaking of the day. And when he saw that he prevailed not against him, he touched the hollow of his thigh; and the hollow of Jacob's thigh was out of joint, as he wrestled with him. And he said, Let me go, for the day breaketh. And he said, I will not let thee go, except thou bless me."

Grandma doesn't cry, but she reaches out to pat my hand, so I know I've done good.

I look at Grandma, holding herself in her girdle with dignity and vigilance, and I know she is proud of me for knowing my verses. But would Grandma have invited me here if she knew the kind of girl I am, if she knew the kinds of rules I am breaking, if she knew I'm not the kind of girl welcome at Jesus's tomb?

I am no longer soft, like Aunt Bernice's polished rocks. I am hard and bony, and Aunt Bernice will never hug me again or send me home with a rock as pretty as me.

I make my small body even smaller in the pew, disappearing behind the folds of Grandma's handbag.

If I'm not seen, I can't be hunted.

Aunt Bernice was loud and large and infinitely braver than I am. What would she think if she could see me now, a hungry girl crouched in a pew?

I feel like I'm choking. Something is pressing down on me, and I gasp like I am drowning. I'm no longer a girl sitting in a pew. I am a gaping mouth. And my gaping mouth can't breathe wrapped in the binds of this intimacy. I don't even know what it is that I'm feeling, only that I can't breathe in the confines of this space. Maybe it's the sisterhood. If so, I don't want anything to do with it.

Not missing Luke is the closest I can get to freedom. But I would wrestle an angel for Aunt Bernice's blessing.

Gooseberry

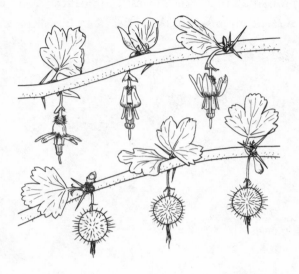

The wild gooseberry is a stout shrub that grows 4 to 6 feet high, with a spread of 3 to 4 feet, with large green, yellow, or purple berries up to an inch in diameter. It is rampant across hills and mountains from 3,500 to 8,500 feet elevation. Gooseberry shrubs are full of thorns—on the branches and sometimes even on the berries themselves.

If you find gooseberries without thorns, you can eat them raw, but the branches will be spiky and may impale your hands, so be careful either way.

If the berries have thorns, boiling them is the best option. When heated, you can smash the berries into a pulp and consume it all: skin, spikes, fruit, and juice.

"ONE OF YOU IS DEFYING our Lord, and he will not be mocked. *Before he formed thee in thy mother's belly, he knew thee, and before thou camest forth out of the womb he sanctified thee.* Come forward now or be cast into the fire . . ."

I assume Mrs. Mitchell means me, but I can't be sure. It is possible there is someone else she's fishing to catch. I have confessed unnecessarily before, and I suspect this is what she wants—as many confessions as she can tease out of us. Whomever she has in mind, she certainly won't speak her name. Not until she gives everyone else a chance to confess their petty crimes (spiritual jealousy, failure to turn in an assignment, not doing the dishes last night, talking to a boy), until she has a chance to peer into the hearts of all of us, until each of us chastises ourselves for causing this rift in our family and confesses.

"If you confess now, God is just and able to forgive . . ."

We are in the mess hall, praying. All twenty-seven teenagers from the Field have come up to our mountain to get away from the world. Part of our education is to learn the biota of the Mountain, and part of it is to become unified in Christ.

Two weeks ago, I was called up to Grandpa's old office, where Mr. Eriksen informed me that Luke had turned in the letters I had written to him over the past year. He praised Luke for turning them in and he said he would hold me responsible for tempting him.

"But," he says, "God has seen to it that the devil has not prevailed."

I don't tell them Luke wrote me first or ask why they don't care about his letters.

"Who do you think you are," Mr. Eriksen asked, "to pave the way to his house with destruction? You are like Jezebel, and your words drip honey while your mouth is smoother than oil."

I know the story of Jezebel, and I don't think there's anything in there about her mouth. I think she made up her eyes to meet her death, as was the custom of her people. I think the mouth part is a reference from Proverbs about an adulteress, which Jezebel was not. But I don't tell him that.

I know I have sinned. Even if no one ever finds out what else Luke and I have done, I have destroyed the unity of our group, and I will be condemned to the fire, where there is weeping and gnashing of teeth.

But it's possible Mr. Eriksen didn't tell either of my parents. Or Mrs. Mitchell. Not to protect me, but to protect them and the system they run. Having a wayward daughter is more than an embarrassment. It's likely a deal breaker. If you can't control your child, how can you control anyone else's? But Mrs. Mitchell may be fishing for someone else this time, so I remain quiet, hoping God will not strike me dead.

I keep my eyes open and watch the other members genuflect to the prayer Mrs. Mitchell is solemnly and soulfully reciting. "Our heavenly Father, thou art so just thou knowest our innermost thoughts. Help these young people to understand that thou died on the cross for them, that your blood can cleanse them, that they can go out and sin no more."

She has addressed this particular prayer to God the Father, not the Son, but she doesn't seem to recognize the contradiction, and no one else seems to notice. No one at the Field except Uncle Stephen makes much of the distinction between God from the Old Testament and Jesus the man, executed by Pontius Pilate. I find this conflation wildly inaccurate, and if I was as disrespectful on the outside as I am on the inside, I would interrupt to ask her to whom we are praying. To whom should I make my case?

Mrs. Mitchell keeps praying to the God who serves her, like she's trying to convince the rest of us it's a good deal. "Help them to rely on each other and realize they cannot make it alone. Help them to see that they need the wisdom of their leaders to make choices. It says in your word that you must lose your life in order to gain it. Help them to see that now is the time to dedicate their lives to your service, for you know that a man who takes his hand to the plow and looketh back is not fit for the kingdom of heaven. We ask this all in thy holy name and for the sake of thy son Jesus Christ. Amen."

People at the Field say God's spirit is like a dove. It flies down gently to land in an open hand. You have to be ready. You don't know when the dove will come to you. If your hand isn't open when it appears, if you don't have the food prepared and waiting, or if you close your hand and try to grab it, the dove will go away. Doves are fragile creatures, and once scorned, they do not come back. If we don't accept God when he comes to us as a dove, we may never have another chance.

They make it sound simple, but it's not. There are a lot of unspoken rules, rules no one has written down, rules you must adhere to or be banished.

Late last night, Luke followed me to the outhouse to tell me he was sorry. It was the first time we'd talked since he turned in the letters, but I wasn't consciously mad at him. Turning the other cheek is what Mother trained me to do, and I do it well. Nevertheless, I wasn't yet ready to tell him that, because forgiveness is akin to weakness around here, and I can't afford to be weak.

"It was too much pressure," he said. "You can't imagine how bad they made me feel for hiding them."

"How'd they know you were hiding them?" I asked.

"Well, they didn't, but they talked so much about the hidden recesses of the heart . . . You know, how the cup is clean and beautiful on the outside, but it's full of dead men's bones inside?"

"Whitewashed tombs."

"What?"

"Whitewashed tombs hold the bones. The cup and dish part's earlier—they're just dirty."

"Whatever. Do you know the verse I'm talking about?"

Of course I knew the verse, but nodding seemed more polite than explaining the Bible.

"They said we were supposed to open ourselves up to the Spirit, and I wanted to, but I didn't have anyone to talk to about it, and I thought your stuff was getting in my way."

My stuff.

He handed me a bouquet of desiccated leaves and berries. "Here," he said. "You can make some jam, like you said you would."

I took them from him, but I didn't tell him they were gooseberries, not chokecherries, and that they look nothing alike and he should know the difference.

"I wanted to do the right thing. They made me feel so guilty . . ."

"Yes, well, they do that. That's their job."

I started to walk up the hill, but I heard Aunt Bernice's voice in my head. *Lord have mercy.*

I stopped.

Luke never raises his voice. He knows how to stroke my hair, like some mothers do with their little girls, making them feel safe and loved. He's an only child, like Dad, and his father is dead, just like Dad's was when he was a teenager. I looked back at him tenderly, realizing this might be the last time we ever talk to each other.

"It's okay," I said. "You did what you had to do. It's okay. I promise."

"What will happen to you?" he asks.

"I'll be okay. Don't worry about me."

I leave the mess hall during Mrs. Mitchell's prayer to wait outside in the hollow of the black oak, anticipating what's next on the agenda, which is most likely me.

If Luke is publicly confronted, he will leave. He says he will stay, that this is his calling to be at the Field for life, that he will take up the cross, but he doesn't know what's about to happen. They will belittle him in front of everyone, and he will become a Quitter—a category of people worse than Outsiders—a group of people I have loathed and condemned all my life. Luke has spent the last several years preparing for the Lord's battle, but he will leave before it begins.

It will be many years before I can forgive myself for tempting him by riding that bike around. Right now, it all feels like my fault.

I sit on my guilty hands to warm them.

Luke doesn't know all the unwritten rules. He wasn't born here, like I was.

What are all these rules? All these codes of behavior I have tried so hard to follow all these years to keep myself open to God. I blow on my hands and start to list them in my notebook.

    1. Thou shalt have no other gods before me, and thou shalt put me and my service above everything else in thy life.

What does this really mean? Infinitely more than faithfully attending Sunday services, or not working for money on the Sabbath, or not going to rock concerts, where people worship graven images. I interpret:

    1. Thou shalt have no other gods before me, and thou shalt put me and my service above everything else in thy life. Thou shalt be on call at all times. Thou shalt not miss a church service, club meeting, camp, trip, game, practice, outing, or other group activity unless thou art considerably ill (with a temperature above 102 degrees).

Is that one category? I read it over. Yes, the idea of commitment is paramount. It captures the spirit of it. The first half of the real Ten Commandments deal with one's relationship to God, and the second half to one's neighbors. People say the commandments were written in order of importance. Commitment is most important. If the Field made a list of its laws, that would definitely be first. But what would be next? Probably respect.

2. Thou shalt not take the name of the Lord thy God in vain, nor use obscene or profane language, including anything that may be interpreted as anything obscene or profane (i.e., gosh, gee, gee whiz, jeez, darn, shoot . . .)

They say God wants us to follow his spirit, not his laws. The rich, young ruler said he had never broken a commandment, and Jesus said that was good but that he must sell all he had and give the money to the poor. God knows where you are weak, the leaders say, and he wants more than obedience. If they wrote down the rules, young people might think following them was enough. But whatever you're doing is not enough, they say. God always wants more.

For example, some of the teenagers brought cassettes of music from their old lives and hid them with their Walkman audio players. I don't have an old life. I've never owned a Walkman or even touched one. My only reference is Mother's clunky old cassette player, which she uses for recording animal sounds. If I had known what Lizbeth and the other righteous teenagers were about to do, I might have pilfered a Billy Joel or Lionel Richie cassette from the stack of cassettes they confiscated, before they burned them all in the campfire last night. I didn't try to stop them, but I didn't participate either. I just listened to the fire from the gully as it made crackling and hissing noises, like the wrath of God.

I think about this as I write down the other basic concepts and try to formulate them into (unwritten) rules.

3. If thy family of origin is not from the Field, thou shalt deny thy family of origin and cleave unto the Field family as thine own.

4. Thou shalt not listen to popular music nor attend movies. (Wholesome plays and hymns are acceptable.)

5. If thou art a boy, thy hair shall be cut above thy ears and thou shalt not wear any form of facial hair. If thou art a girl, thou shalt not wear trendy clothes or hairstyles, or skirts that reveal thy knees, nor shalt thou unbutton thy blouse more than one inch below the base of thy neck.

6. Thou shalt not imbibe, inhale, or refer to any mind-altering substance for as long as thou shalt live.

7. Thou shalt not dance.

8. Thou shalt not fraternize with anyone outside of the Field except to obtain money.

9. Thou shalt not touch anyone of the opposite sex in any manner until thou meeteth them at the altar in marriage.

10. Thou shalt not deeply connect or become infatuated with any human.

Have I gotten it right? I reread my list to check for details. I scratch out a few words and substitute others. Put God first, think holy thoughts, never participate in sensual desires of the flesh. Yes, that about covers it.

I put my hands between my thighs again to warm them, and I like the way it feels to have them there.

I will bear the entire brunt of the seduction of Luke, and I envision a year of banishment versus a lifetime of excommunication. This meeting will start it all off. With pressure from the leaders, the entire group will intimidate Luke. He will leave the meeting as if in defeat, though probably in relief, and then I will be left with the fallout.

As Grandpa's seed, I am the bridge to the future, and breaking my spirit will benefit them all. Banishing me is the best object lesson available, and they will not hesitate to use it. I have nowhere to go. I can't name one person outside the Field who would take me in. They will expect me to capitulate, to apologize and beg for reinstatement. They will want me to promise that nothing like this will ever happen again, perform the restitution of working menial tasks for months in silence, without social acknowledgment, and sign a life pledge when I'm eighteen.

Sometimes banished members stick it out in limbo for a few months, pulling weeds in the back forty, cleaning bathrooms, and hosing out trash cans. They put in the same hours of service as the rest of the community (twelve-hour days, seven days a week), but no one is allowed to talk to them. If they continue to show up and complete their work, without complaint, they can hope for eventual reinstatement on a trial basis. They would no longer have the honor of coaching teams or teaching students, and they would no longer vote on issues, but they would be able to stay at the Field, in the circle of God's care.

If you endure banishment and are reinstated, it's not the same as excommunication. But you'll never be fully respected or trusted again.

Luke walks out of the mess hall without looking at me and heads toward the A-frames.

They call me in. I listen and surmise that the question at hand is whether I wrote the seductive letters. They don't know about the candy or the hospital or the nights we spent looking at the moon. They know only about the thirty-four letters he turned in.

I want those letters back.

Everyone must choose a side. The leaders pretend it's a sort of jury, that my peers are voting on whether I have written the letters and thereby committed the crime of seduction. But if you don't vote the way the leaders want you to, you are excommunicated. It's always this way. The leaders say they are only judges, appointed by God to determine sentencing. But in reality, they are the lawyers, who interpret Grandpa's unwritten laws, the jury, who determines whether we've broken these nebulous rules, the judges, who provide sentencing, and the correction officers, who maintain the boundaries of the closed community, keeping us in, or escorting us out.

"Sometimes she smiles and moves her hair in a way God doesn't approve of. That's evidence enough."

"Yes, I have seen that."

"I agree."

"She uses her body for attention, when she should be denying herself to be in the body of Christ."

"Who else would write thirty-four letters?"

"She will be better off when she realizes she is not special."

Not special. No, no. No one is special. There is no one who cannot be replaced. *We are all paper cups.*

What would they do to me if I tried to rebel, if I refused to follow the mandated codes of public behavior? I carry around my private thoughts like a cloak, thinking there's a part of me they can't reach. What would they do if I ran away before they could condemn me?

"Yeah, she wrote them for sure."

"I agree."

What will Lizbeth say? Will they let my sister abstain?

"I think Michelle needs to understand the weight of her transgression," she says. "We can't always do what we want in life. We can't follow desire, like little children do. Christ says we must give up this world for the one hereafter. I want to do what's best for my sister and save her soul." Lizbeth looks at me. "Who do you think you are?" she asks. "Do you think you can keep from sinning without our support? Do you think you are so strong you can lead a godly life without this group? Who do you think you are?"

It will not be a question of whether or not I will stay but how I will endure their rejection. They want me to be ashamed. They want me to say I'm sorry, to plead for reinstatement, to give up every part of myself and move to the rhythm of the group.

I can't imagine what I can possibly do to prevent all this. I look over at the kitchen and picture Luke making mashed potatoes, stirring in chunks of government butter. He will leave, and he will not take me with him. I will never escape the Field, and I will never escape my hunger.

Grandpa's followers are still talking when I walk out. No one follows me as I make my way down to the house and into my mother's secret drawer, where she keeps pills in a bottle to combat the pain that comes with being a woman. She doesn't offer them to us during our times of the month, but I've seen her take them and she's more relaxed after.

I pour myself a large glass of water and take a bunch of her pills.

I am going to hell eventually. Might as well do it on my own terms. I feel one pill lodged in my throat. Maybe more than one. I feel as if they are mounting, as if they are stacked on top of one another, beginning in my stomach, filling my esophagus, scaling my throat. I drink more water and take more pills. I instinctively gag and feel the thick, warm saliva run down my chin. I struggle to hold back the vomit. My eyes burn, and I bite my lip in relief; they are still in there. I will not have to do this again.

I go back to my bunk, hoping it will not be long. I look up at the pines, rustling in the cool mountain air, and wonder if the meeting is over. It pains me that I won't see Luke again, but I would rather die than watch him walk away and leave me here. To be held like that and then to be let go is not something I can bear. The first time he told me he loved me, I couldn't breathe from the knot wedged so tight in my throat. I lie in my sleeping bag waiting for the symptoms, whatever they will be—blurry vision, headache, dizziness—whatever will happen before I sink into a deep, sweet sleep.

"Michelle, are you okay? It's time for dinner."

It's my friend Angela's voice, and she sounds like she's talking to her Baby Alive doll from long ago. "It's time for dinner," she says, and I think, *Yes, I know. We should go, shouldn't we? But let's not. Don't leave. Just stay here and fall asleep with me like you used to.*

She is touching me, I think. I think she is climbing up on the bunk with me. *Thank you, Angela. Thank you for coming back for me.* She tells me it's not that bad, that I'm still allowed to eat with them, that I just need to come in now before I get her in trouble.

I face away from her so she won't see my sadness. How far will I go before God turns me into a pillar of salt?

"I'm all filled up," I mumble, pulling my head in tighter within my sleeping bag, shivering. I breathe her in and tell myself I need to turn away. She is reminding me of how cold I am, how freezing everything in my life feels, how impossible it feels to ever thaw.

"You can't stay here," she says. "It's against the rules."

She's pulling on me, but my head is too heavy to lift. I give in to whatever she is doing to me, and then somehow we both fall onto the dirt with a thud.

She is yelling then, and I hear their voices, all their swimming voices. I am underwater, I think, but I can hear them out there, muffled, but comprehensible. There are bright lights in my eyes, bright lights through the trees, bright lights pulsating red and white, fire and ice. Is this my Damascus?

"How much does she weigh?"

"One hundred twenty pounds."

"Oh, no, she's much lighter than that . . ."

"It doesn't matter. They just want a range."

They don't know how much I weigh. My father, ruler of weekly weigh-ins, hasn't passed on his supreme knowledge, after all.

"Ask her which pills and how many."

"She's unconscious."

"Is she?"

"It doesn't matter. She's not talking."

"Why wouldn't she talk?"

So many voices. I can't tell any of them apart.

"What'd he do to her?"

"Who?"

"Forget it."

"Who's she talking about?"

"They said they're coming. Leave her where she is. Clear out all the other members."

"Everyone, there's been an emergency. Get your jackets and go to chapel."

In the ambulance, a man makes me drink a thick liquid that tastes like gooseberries, only sweeter. I drink most of it and push the rest away, but he says, "No, drink it all."

When we arrive at the hospital in Loma Linda, my stomach is pumped.

Instead of admitting me as an inpatient, a woman escorts me from the emergency room to a psychiatric ward, following a California law that requires minors who have attempted suicide to receive psychiatric analysis before they are released. I am uncomfortable with the term *psychiatric analysis* and the way the woman looks at me, but I listen to her when she explains the procedure.

I pause and glance through the small observation windows cut high up into the doors as they walk me down the hall, taking note of the pink rooms and the huddled patients in the corners, wondering if they will keep me here, wondering if this is where I belong.

She speaks kindly to me, asking me to wait a few minutes while she does some paperwork. I sit still and listen to the nurses talk, like I've always listened to them talk when they think no one is listening. She comes back and says I'm in luck, that the doctor can see me in a few minutes, and that he'll decide what we do next.

I ask her if I can use the bathroom. She says yes, and I lock myself in for a few private moments. I look down at my stomach, gloriously flat, and I touch it where it aches from the hours of vomiting. My throat is raw, my head throbs, and I have to put my hand out on the wall to steady myself. I wrap my arms around my middle and hug myself until my knees feel less weak. *What to do, what to do?* I press my forehead to the door and bang it softly. *What to do, what to do?* I pucker my lips and flatten them against the wood. *Don't leave me, don't leave me, don't leave me.*

I hear my name being called. I pull myself together and go out to meet the nurse, who escorts me into an office and closes the door on her way out. This is a different kind of room than I've ever been in with a doctor. An old man sits behind a desk in a suit, and he asks me how I'm feeling.

"Good," I say, smiling at him. "I'm sorry for taking up your time at the end of your shift. I'm sure you're exhausted from being here all day."

He says he doesn't mind, then asks me questions about my family, and I say what I think I should say: that it's hard seeing your way out of problems sometimes, but that hospitals have mostly been good to me.

I talk about being sick growing up and feeling alienated. I don't talk about Grandpa or my uncles or the seven seals or the colors of the horses that will usher in our tribulations. He speaks kindly to me, but he's still an Outsider, and Outsiders aren't to be trusted.

"How's your family?" I ask. "Is it hard on them when you work late?"

"I don't think you wanted to die," he says, ignoring my questions. "I think you just wanted to get away for a while. Does that sound true to you?"

I don't know what's true. I just want to protect my family. *Wherefore take unto you the whole armour of God, that ye may be able to withstand in the evil day, and having done all, to stand. Stand therefore, having your loins girt about with truth.*

He asks me what I'm good at, what I'm proud of.

"Pride goeth before destruction, and a haughty spirit before a fall," I say without thinking.

"You seem like a smart girl. May I be frank with you?"

I look at him. I'm not used to adults asking my opinion before declaring orders. He reminds me of Dr. Shore, except older.

"You look open and friendly, but I think your smile is a well-rehearsed defense mechanism," he says.

He looks at me, perhaps waiting for a response, but I don't give one.

"I think that smile has protected you so many times you use it when you're angry and scared and hurt and hungry. I think you are telling me what you think I want to hear, but I am hearing something else."

I smile, waiting for him to tell me what he hears.

"I'm hearing something you can't tell me and can't tell yourself. That smile is protecting you from something you're not going to tell me about today. It might take several sessions to even begin to get you to talk about what you're not even allowing yourself to think about, and I don't see regular clients right now, so I can't even offer you that." He pauses, watching me closely. "We need to make a choice here, and I want you to help me make this choice. I can admit you to this facility for care, which will get you away from the people who are undoubtedly hurting you, but that comes with a price. You'll become part of a system, and, as you well know, it's hard to get out of a system."

I smile. The doctor smiles back. Neither of us say anything for at least a minute.

"So I'm going to give you the choice," he says, "and I want you to think about it before you answer." He looks at me, and I nod, to show I'm listening. "There is easily enough evidence to keep you here. We can hospitalize you and treat you here and then move you into a foster family. But at sixteen, this will not be a permanent arrangement, so you will be physically safe but unmoored. Or you can tell me you're not going to do this again. You can assure me you will hold out a few more months, apply to college, get a scholarship, and get out of whatever situation has left you feeling that dying is better than fighting. If I let you go, I will mandate counseling. But, most importantly, I need to know what you want. Do you want to stay here and start this process, or do you want to go back? And if you go back, can you assure me you have enough inner resources to hold on until you can get into college?"

I don't want to go to college. I feel flattened by the weight of the world, by the expanse of buildings full of people I don't understand, who move and speak and act in ways I can't predict. I want to stay here. I want to choose what I know. I want to stay in a hospital forever and ever. Doing what I know doesn't feel like choosing. It just feels safe.

But I want to understand the implications of what he is offering me.

"Can you give me an example of an inner resource and how I would use it?" I ask.

He smiles in a way that lights him up from the inside, so that I can see his light from over here. "The way you listen is a resource," he says. "Your intelligence. Your vocabulary. What if you write down the conversations you listen to, word for word, like dialogue, instead of taking them personally?"

I already do that, but he's suggesting I can do more, that I can keep gnawing my way through this, that what I've been doing is a form of survival.

I tell him I will stay alive long enough to find my way out. And I do.

Later, when I have left religion behind, I will look back at this conversation and fall on my knees, offering a prayer of gratitude to a God I no longer believe in. And I will think of the insolence, cunning, and fierceness I learned from the stories of Rahab, Tamar, and Ruth, and I will bless my dear dead grandma for teaching me what survival looks like for women like us.

The prospect of going back doesn't terrify me the way it would have if the doctor hadn't validated my ability to forage.

Mother doesn't speak while we're getting in the car. I lie down on the back seat and pretend to sleep, but the car doesn't start. I turn toward the front and am assaulted by Mother's face, mere inches above me, long and drawn and twisted in judgment.

"You embarrass me," she says, "but you'll go back to class tomorrow and act like nothing happened."

Mother starts driving, and I breathe to the rhythm of the wheels. Part of me wants to tell her I had an epiphany—that Christ showed himself to me last night, that this experience has been my Damascus and I will give up living in the flesh— because I know that will make her happy. I want to tell her I will dedicate myself to the Field, that I don't need anything, that I will be a follower and go out and sin no more, so that she will feel satisfied and leave me alone.

But I don't say that. I don't say anything at all.

"Don't tell your father," she says.

I sit up and look out the window, just as the sun is peeking up over Mormon Rocks. As we drive through the high desert, I see swaths of yucca arising with the sun. I will never tell my father anything.

The Lord's candles shine bright against the rocky sand, lit like flames rising up from the depths of destruction. I am drawn to them like a moth, seeking connection, imagining that the light can lead me home.

Knobcone Pine

The knobcone is a small pine tree, 10 to 30 feet tall, with yellow-green needles in groups of threes. It grows in the poorest of soils, up to 7,000 feet elevation, and reseeds only after a fire.

Knobcone bark and needles are tough and fibrous and hard to digest, and its cones are hard to access, staying tightly closed until they reach a temperature of about 400 degrees Fahrenheit, at which point the sap in the cones begins to loosen and they release their stored seeds.

Harvesting seeds from a knobcone takes more knowledge and skill than from any other pine tree, especially if you have *no tools to work with. You won't be able to extract the seeds without extreme heat.*

THE SUMMER I AM SIXTEEN, I know all the routes through Arcadia, Monrovia, Rosemead, and Sierra Madre. I ride the bike I have not yet returned to Tammy to every housecleaning job I have acquired, tracing the route of the Night Stalker, who, for the past few months, has been climbing in windows murdering people in the cities in which I live and work.

Danny and our parents are with the boys on the Trip, and Lizbeth is on the Mountain, cooking for the campers who have come up to turn their back on the world and pray. Aunt Mildred is moving somewhere no one will talk about, and soon, Lizbeth will move into Grandma's house full-time to take care of her.

I'm not allowed to be on the Mountain, because I can't be trusted. And I'm not allowed to go over to Grandma's anymore either, because Mother says it's too much for her to have to put up with the kind of drama I bring.

I suspect Mother is right on this one. Grandma doesn't deserve what I have put her through, with my years of sickness and my inability to follow rules. Her hold on reality is slim now, and my relationship with Grandpa's followers is troublesome enough to cause her distress.

Becca is staying at the Mitchells' house while Mr. Mitchell is on the Trip. Mrs. Mitchell is trying to keep Becca from turning to the dark side, so she is forbidden to talk to me. I understand this rule, but I miss her. She's the only piece of my family I still feel connected to. Becca isn't allowed to answer their phone, because it's not her house, but sometimes I call anyway, especially when I think Mrs. Mitchell won't be at home. Sometimes Mrs. Mitchell answers, and when she hears my voice, she hangs up on me, like it's a wrong number. Sometimes it rings over and over and over, and I just sit there listening to the rhythm of rejection.

But I keep trying, because I love Becca, even though we don't say that to each other. We've both learned to deny our needs, but the reaching for each other is mutual, and we depend on one another, even through wires of silence. The rules we're required to follow keep us apart but can't entirely sever our connection.

I am living with the Anderson family on the Field's bank and riding Tammy's bike through the suburbs in search of a narrative I can adopt as my own. I'm looking for markers and boundaries to attach to, ones I can use to make sense of a widening world. My cognitive map feels disembodied away from the Mountain. I can get where I need to go, but I never seem to know where I am.

The Andersons have three sons a little younger than I am, and four or five boys in their early twenties living in the back quarters. It is hot in the Andersons' house, because we have a lot of bodies sleeping in here without an air conditioner, and we can't open any windows because of the Night Stalker.

Mrs. Anderson is one of the women who used to take care of Lizbeth and me on and off when we were babies, and I think she's a little stunned by how big I've grown. She tells me it has been many years since she has lived with a girl, and she apologizes for not knowing what I need. I am jarred by this word, *need*. I don't have any idea what she's talking about.

Mrs. Anderson presses chocolate-chip cookie dough into large pans, cooks it like cake, and cuts it into bars. She wraps them in plastic wrap and stacks them in the freezer, so that the boys can have a homemade cookie with milk anytime they want. I watch Mr. Anderson come in and warm one in the microwave. He sits down with milk. Their sons do the same.

I take a cookie whenever I want one, but I eat them frozen, so that I don't have to spend any time in the kitchen or draw attention to myself. Sometimes I eat them while I ride to my cleaning jobs.

I am still obsessed with staying thin, certain that I can't turn into a woman if I can keep my breasts from growing. I am accustomed to living on sugar, so low-grade nausea has become a state of being for me. One week, to keep my calories to a minimum, I eat nothing but frozen cookies.

Mrs. Anderson doesn't ask me anything about my days or where I go on the bike. She just asks me to be home by dark, which is easy to do on summer nights, because the sun sets so late and no one wants me cleaning at night anyway.

At night, I sit next to the closed window and look out at the street, writing long letters to Luke that I will never send. I use a thesaurus and practice finding words that capture the nuance of what I'm trying to say, clarifying my thoughts for myself, more than for him. I don't want to admit to myself that I love him, because along with love comes need, and I don't want to have needs. If I rely on him, he can disappoint me, and I can't endure the thought of any more of that. I write letters saying things I would say if I didn't have to hide, and in thinking about what that requires, I find a sort of truth. And the truth is, I'd rather be killed by the Night Stalker than live in the world as I know it.

I want to climb out and look at the moon, but the Night Stalker has attacked more than a dozen people in our area since March. All the women at all my jobs know all the details of the past four months of killings, and they talk about them so often I have the victims memorized. In March, two were in Rosemead, one in Monterey Park, and two in Whittier. Since May, the killings have been closer to us. Last month in Monrovia, where I frequently work, two women were found bludgeoned in their bedrooms, and this month, the Night Stalker beat a woman and slashed her throat in Arcadia, where I live with the Andersons. In the past two weeks, a sixteen-year-old girl escaped his attack in Sierra Madre, but two women in Monterey Park were raped, sodomized, and then beaten (one to death), before he shot a couple in Glendale and killed a family of three.

Grandpa had warned all about this kind of thing, so maybe the end of the world is really nigh and we will soon be running to the hills. I feel more prepared for the hills than I do for the life I'm living here. The Night Stalker doesn't seem to follow girls around during the day, so there's some freedom when its light, but at night, we are all trapped inside, in case this whole murdering spree is not part of God's plan.

The Mountain feels far away, much too far away to run to. So I stay up all night writing letters I will never send, watching the shadows of the streetlamps on the empty asphalt, making sure no one climbs through any windows at this house on my watch.

I like the people at most of my jobs. Whether they are present when I clean or just leave me notes with instructions, I get insights into their worlds from working in the intimacy of their living spaces, broadening my comprehension of home.

The women whose homes I clean comment on the sophistication of my vocabulary. Some of them say my voice has an accent, or an unusual cadence they can't place. They ask me where I come from. I want to say, "Somewhere you haven't heard of," but mostly I say, "All over."

They ask me where I will go to college. I shrug and ask them where they went to college. Some of them tell me where they graduated from and some tell me where they were when they dropped out, and I notice that they all have a college story and light up when they tell it.

Sometimes I stay after and read to their children or help them write thank-you notes for the gifts they've received at extravagant birthday parties I can't envision. Word spreads among the mothers, and soon I have several jobs tutoring children in reading and vocabulary, some of them at houses I don't even clean.

No one at the Field talks to me except the Anderson family, and mostly only because we all share a bathroom and have to make room for one another.

Mrs. Anderson gives me a little package of Avon makeup samples she gets from a saleswoman who comes to the house when I'm not there. I learn to paint the rims of my eyes in blue, so I look like the women at the homes I visit, not the ones I know at the Field.

One of my longest jobs is with a woman named Mrs. Stewart. She's been a housewife her whole adult life, so she's almost always there, married to her house. She follows me around and sometimes she tells me stories about her husband, whom she doesn't always like.

She cleans every day, so there really isn't anything that needs to be done when I'm there once a week, but she asks me to do the things that are hard for her, like scrub the bathroom floors on my hands and knees with a rag, getting into every crevice. And she teaches me to do what she calls "tedious chores," like using a screwdriver to gently remove the mirrored glass compartments from her jewelry box and clean both sides before I screw them back in. I rub each piece of her jewelry until it shines, and I lay it down on a mirror on the counter, so the jewels reflect fragments of light across my face.

I have never known a woman with so much time on her hands, nor anyone who cares so much about detail, but I have worked for her for almost a year, and I have become accustomed to her rhythms and her desires. And even though she is at least forty years older than me and monitors every single moment of my work like a hawk, she treats me like a friend.

A couple hours into each of my workdays, she says I need a break, and even though I really don't, I'm on her clock, so I do as she says. She pours me exactly half a can of 7Up and pours herself the other half, and we sit at her kitchen table, and she compliments the texture and color of my hair and tells me things she thinks I should know, like how to be the kind of woman a man wants to take care of, how expensive jewelry and perfumes signal value and make a man think you're worth investing in. As I listen to her, I start to think that the bottles of L'Air du Temps and Anaïs Anaïs she gave me for Christmas feel consecrated and a little like love.

One day, she sets up a slide projector, and she fills each slot with a miniature picture. She clicks through them, one by one, and shows me where she and Mr. Stewart went on their last vacation. I sip my 7Up slowly, because she does.

I don't know any of the countries she is naming, but they are all places in Europe. There are paintings and food and lots of books. I ask her questions, and that makes her happy. We spend an hour on this break instead of the allotted fifteen minutes, and she tells me I am a smart girl and I should go to college. I tell her maybe I will.

Today Mrs. Stewart greets me and asks me to help make her pretty. She says they are going to the racetrack and she needs to look her best. I help her curl the back of her hair and bobby-pin her hat in place so it won't be taken by the wind. I do her eye makeup and help her match her lipstick to the manicure she had done yesterday. She spins around for me, asking for my final approval, and I clap. She smiles at me and leaves cash for me on the counter as she leaves, reminding me to lock the door on my way out.

I turn the dial on her stereo and listen to her cassette of Phil Collins, singing along as I work. I am in the bathroom cleaning her jewelry box when I hear the front door open.

I freeze and stop singing, but I can't stop the stereo without being seen, so Phil Collins keeps going, creating a soundtrack for whatever is about to happen next.

I stand there, wondering what to do, when I see Mr. Stewart in the doorway. He smells weird. Something in him, or on him, fills the bathroom with a sour stench, a little like morning breath mixed with body odor, or maybe more like a public bathroom that hasn't been cleaned. I am thinking about how to describe this when Mr. Stewart says, "Come here," motioning with two of his fingers in a way that looks ridiculous to me. There are different kinds of predators in the suburbs.

"I have to clean these things. Mrs. Stewart will be angry at me if I don't finish my work," I say, because it's my job to be polite. Then I keep talking, because Mother taught me to always have something to say, and maybe this is why. "Is she still at the race? I thought you were there with her. Which horse won? Did you bet on that horse?"

He takes a step toward me, reaches out, and grabs my arm, pulling me into his smelly body, my breasts pressed up against his belly, my face smashed into his chest. He reaches for my sweatpants and starts to pull them down. No one has done this since I was seven, and standing here against his large body makes me feel like a little girl. He smells like apples and vomit and Frank.

I want to scream, but I get very calm, because he is much bigger than me. I don't threaten him with the screwdriver, but I don't let it go either.

I use my hands, one of which is holding the screwdriver, to push lightly against his stomach, freeing my face, so that I can look up at him and smile.

"It's good to see you!" I say in my most reverential voice.

My back is pressed against the bathroom counter, and his large body stands between me and the door. I lift myself on tiptoe and give him a kiss on the cheek. "Let me get you a 7Up!" I say.

He doesn't move, but the wedge I've created with my kiss gives me enough space to fall to my knees and scramble past him into the hallway toward the kitchen, where I grab the money Mrs. Stewart has left, then run out the front door, where Tammy's bike is parked.

I ride away on my strong legs, the screwdriver still in my hand.

I can't imagine going back to all the boys at the Anderson house, so I ride to Grandma's house instead, my legs soft and squishy, like a melted candy bar. I knock on her door and wait.

She doesn't answer, so I ring the doorbell and wait a little longer. After one more try, I put the screwdriver between my teeth, so that my hands are free to climb the fence, and I crawl through the dog door. Then I head straight to Aunt Mildred's old room and try the doorknob.

It opens.

I stand at the door and survey the empty room. It's smaller than I thought. Maybe eight by ten feet, just large enough to hold the bed and the rocking chair Mildred has left behind. Lizbeth's yellow suitcase is in the closet, but there is nothing else here. I lock the door from the inside and test it. Aunt Mildred's lock still works.

I put the screwdriver in my pocket and assess the scene. There are two windows, one facing the street and the other facing a brick wall on the side that borders another Field family. In front of the cinder-block wall is a patch of grass covered in dandelions and a solitary rosebush, desiccated from lack of care. I stare out at the grass and the dried rosebuds clinging to the almost-barren bush. I try to open the window, but it doesn't budge.

I pound the glass, which shakes the wall but still doesn't open the window. Part of me wants to shatter the glass, but it is double-paned and heavy and doesn't care how I feel. I know I should stop hitting it, since I might be alerting Grandma to my presence, but I can't stop. I keep pounding the glass, angry at it for not yielding to my power.

I think of Dad and his physical power, the way he used to slam doors or punch his fist into the wall, leaving holes in the drywall that we never seemed to fix. I think of his bouts of rage, some of which were directed at us, and I wonder if he, too, is sequestered in a world he can't fix, reaching for what he wants, separated from whatever relatives he once had, trapped in a marriage that yokes him to a family that will never be his own.

For the first time, I feel like my father's daughter.

I think of using the rocking chair to bludgeon the window until it breaks. Instead, I press my face flat on the cloudy glass and stare at the dried buds. *I could make tea with those buds,* I think. *I could boil water and make dandelion and rose-hip tea.*

I sit down on the bed, discouraged. The screwdriver presses against my buttocks. I stand up and take it out of my pocket and fondle the handle, looking at the small, flat edge.

And I have a better idea. I press it under the edge of the sill, where the wood of the window and the framing meet, sliding it roughly along the paint. It doesn't make a dent. I pound it in harder, to make an impression. Nothing.

I can't breathe in this stuffy room. I can't breathe in this stuffy life. I want those dandelions. I want those rose hips. I want nourishment, and I want a mother.

I fall to my knees on the floor of my aunt's abandoned room and hyperventilate. I am hungry, but I've given up on food. I want a paper bag to breathe into.

I want a mother.

When I was born, Mother didn't offer me her breast. She told me she didn't have time for that. "And anyway, my milk never came in," she said. "You were taken to the nursery before I even saw you, because you were allergic to the eye drops they gave you and broke out in hives." She says they didn't give me to her until she went home, and she went back to work at the Field the next day.

I was covered in hives and sickly, an ugly baby, resistant to the formula the hospital sent home with them. Unlike Lizbeth, who was a good baby, Mother says I caused them all endless grief. I cried all the time and wouldn't eat, or I vomited what they tried to feed me. Mother left formula with Mrs. Anderson or whomever else would come over, a rotating cast of followers who had nowhere else to go. I was nurtured by a host of exiles. At night, when she would come home, she would let me cry myself to sleep, so I would get hungry enough to eat. But still, I would resist the plastic nipple and throw up whatever she managed to get down me.

"Eventually, we had to take you to the hospital. They said you were allergic to milk, and we had to buy some special soy powder. That solved the eating. But you were always a difficult child, demanding and never satisfied."

What I hear is, I am inherently unlovable. If I were lovable, she would have loved me. If I were lovable, she would have stayed home this summer. If even my mother can't love me, I can't be loved.

But Lord have mercy, I will breathe.

I scrape the edges with the screwdriver and the paint falls off in little flakes. I poke and prod and pry and press until I find the most effective method of chipping away at the yellow paint. It's slow work, but I am determined. I'm not satisfied with my life, but what can I do about that right now? The only thing that seems possible to change is this window.

I hear Grandma moving around the house, doing her nightly routine. I pause, worried that the noise will scare her, but maybe if I scrape gently, she won't notice.

When I think she is finally asleep, I begin again more vigorously, poking and prodding and prying and pressing, maneuvering into all the little crevices where the dry paint has been solidifying all these years. I don't care how long this takes. I keep chipping away at the paint.

I will get this window open. I will get this window open. I won't stop until I get this window open. I prod to the rhythm. *Open. Open. Open.*

I stand on the rocking chair and tug at the top of the frame, pulling it up toward me. It creaks, but it doesn't give. I think of knobcones, which are serotinous pine cones, needing fire to open and release their seeds. I consider setting the window frame on fire, like Mildred always said I would do.

Or maybe it's the bush out there I should set to flame, so I can hear God's voice: *I am that I am.*

I step back down onto the floor and wield the screwdriver like a spear, pounding it into the wood frame without precision or regard for its well-being.

Eventually, I feel it give way, and I hoist the window open. I am confronted by the night air. There isn't a screen, so I am face-to-face with the night, an opening that feels like home.

I crawl outside and lay my unloved body across the grass.

Once I catch my breath, I kneel and begin to pick the dandelions. I have no pockets, so I fill the front of my shirt so full I have to fold it up and hold it like a hammock, exposing my bra. Without my hands free, I can't cull from the rosebush, so I let my shirt go and the dandelions scatter.

I start over, this time filling my bra. It's late now, and the Night Stalker is probably on his route. I don't have any candy, so if he comes to me now, there will be no kindness. I will stab him straight through the eyes with this screwdriver. I will make him suffer, like the martyrs for Christ.

These aren't mountain rose hips, but they will do. I have to be careful, or the thorns will pierce me. Without gloves, it takes concentration to deftly pick each rose hip off the bush, but of course, some of the thorns pierce me, and I don't flinch.

When my bra is stuffed, I climb back inside and sit on the bed. I don't want to risk waking Grandma by going into the kitchen. I can make the tea tomorrow. I'm tired, and my body feels wounded in a way that needs rest. I have no other clothes here, so I sleep in what I have on, the dandelions and rose hips pressed tight against my heart.

I smell her in my dream, a child drenched in seawater, her hair tangled by the ocean waves. I smell her before I see her, a little blond toddler girl alone on the beach. I see her from the balcony where I am housecleaning for a family. She looks like a small animal down there on the pale sand. I scan the horizon, wondering who she belongs to, worried, because no one is around. I walk down the cliff to go to her, but as I search the empty sand, I can't see her anywhere. Then I see something light bobbing in the ocean, what looks like a little girl's feet, and I run closer, realizing she is facedown in the ocean, floating like a corpse. So I run to her. But just as I am about to dive under a wave to get to her, she starts swimming. I swim after her, as fast as I can, and I reach out and scoop her up, and miraculously, she lets me. She is cold and rigid to the touch and is coughing and spitting up water as I bring her to shore.

I carry her to the house, and I put her in a warm bath and feed her animal crackers and soup. She looks at me with her wide eyes, but she doesn't speak. She seems so cautious, so skeptical, so old.

I wake up hungry for animal crackers, but even if Grandma has some, I don't think they will satiate my hunger. I open my eyes. Something in me has been jolted ajar, and the light is so bright it hurts.

I have left the window open.

California Black Oak

The California black oak is a large deciduous nut tree with shiny green leaves with scalloped edges. It is native to the West Coast and grows best on south-facing slopes, near Jeffrey pines.

The black oak is a wildlife support species, providing food and shelter to a host of animals, including numerous species of birds, squirrels, and chipmunks. It grows in a wide range of habitats, including mixed evergreen forests, oak savannas, and coniferous forests, and is slow-growing, strong, sturdy, and self-sufficient.

The large acorns of the black oak were a staple food for early Americans, who would leach them to remove tannins. To do so, you can boil them, run water over them, or leave *them in a bag in a stream, as Native Americans did. Once leached, they have a mild, potato-like flavor and can be eaten raw, roasted, or ground into flour. Acorns are rich in complex carbohydrates, minerals, oils, fiber, and vitamins.*

I MOVE THROUGH THE MOTIONS of my life, but I am an imposter in my body, the boundaries of which no longer make sense to me. I can't tell where I begin or end in relation to anything in my immediate environment. I can't feel my heartbeat or my breath. I can't tell what is hot or cold, can't detect the temperature of the air or food or water, and when I touch what I think is my skin, I can't feel the relationship between what is doing the touching and what is being touched. I think I may be disintegrating.

I can't go back to the Stewarts, and I'm scared to go back to any of the other jobs, because all of them are connected, one way or another.

I don't know who I am anymore, and I don't know what I was doing at all those houses with all those families who aren't mine. I used to know who I was. I used to have a center, some solid part inside of me that held me together, but now it's as if my core has been shivered to pieces, my insides relegated to a cloud of dust, amorphous and indistinguishable. I feel connected to nothing, which makes me connected to everything. I breathe in the sky. I breathe out dust.

Go to now, ye that say, To day or to morrow we will go into such a city, and continue there a year, and buy and sell, and get gain: Whereas ye know not what shall be on the morrow. For what is your life? It is even a vapour, that appeareth for a little time, and then vanisheth away.

The summer is over. The Night Stalker has been caught. My parents are back from the Trip, and I go back and forth from the Mountain, sometimes staying there, sometimes sleeping down here at whichever Field houses will accept me, since I'm not allowed to stay at Grandma's.

I sneak into Grandma's anyway, of course, learning what it is to be a woman from reading the magazines she keeps out for her piano students.

I turn seventeen sitting on Grandma's couch with Little One and Sois, reading every Can This Marriage Be Saved? column from *Ladies' Home Journal*. The experts pretend they are being objective, but whatever is wrong in the marriages is always the woman's fault.

Submit yourselves therefore to God. Resist the devil, and he will flee from you. Draw nigh to God, and he will draw nigh to you. Cleanse your hands, ye sinners; and purify your hearts, ye double minded. Be afflicted, and mourn, and weep: let your laughter be turned to mourning, and your joy to heaviness.

I want to pound the piano, smash the windows, break the spine and ribs of this house, break the pillars like Samson, and fell the temple, killing everyone inside.

In spring, when the weather warms again, I ride Tammy's bike through the suburban streets, searching for a sign.

I pull into the parking lot of 7-Eleven to look for candy, and I see a Quitter. I've always wondered what it feels like to be a Quitter, but I can't ask him. I'm not supposed to talk to Quitters. I try to avoid his eyes, but he recognizes me.

"Michelle?" Kevin asks, as if he's seeing an apparition. "What are you doing away from the Field?"

It has been only a year since he left, and even though he was once like a brother to me, we are strangers to each other now. I'm speechless, but I'm not sure if that's because I shouldn't be talking to him or because I'm startled I still have a name and that he's used it.

"What are you doing here?" I ask, avoiding his question.

"I live at UC Irvine now, but I'm here visiting my mom."

Living at college is the worst thing a young person can do, we've been told. It ruins you for life.

"How's your mom?" I ask.

Kevin tells me about her work and how it's hard for her without him around, and he asks about my parents and my Grandma, and I smile and tell him the kind of polite things I used to say to the women I worked for, when I had jobs.

"Do you want a ride?" he asks. "We can put your bike here," he says, motioning toward the back of his car.

I stare at his car and I stare at him, and I don't know who I am or why I'm in this parking lot or what I should do next.

He asks me if I'd like to go to the movie theater with him. He has an assignment to read *The Color Purple*, and that there's a movie about it, and he says we can get candy and popcorn and it will be fun.

I stand there smiling at him, suspended between information and incomprehension, both knowing and not knowing what he is offering. I don't know how to respond.

"The movie just came out," he explains. "It's a world that doesn't make sense to me, but maybe the movie will help me understand the book." He laughs. "You're smart. You could help me figure out what's going on. I'll take you to dinner after, and we can talk about it."

"I haven't read the book," I say.

"You will."

I know I shouldn't go with him. But he has a car. It's a sign.

We sit close in the dark, but he doesn't touch me. As the music starts, he warns me I will see things that make me uncomfortable. I hunch down, preparing for darkness.

What I'm not prepared for is the light. I had no idea this evil thing I had been warned about doing could be so luminous. The movie is long, full of heartache and alienation, but also community and love and loyalty. I'm transported by the music and the landscape and the familiarity of the sisterhood. I don't eat the candy Kevin has given me, because that would pull me into here instead of there. And right now, there is no place I would rather be than inside the lives of these women who show up for one another in a way that is forbidden where I come from. Of course, it's forbidden in their world too. They're just more courageous than I am.

I watch, and I weep.

While the credits roll, Kevin reaches for my hand, and I feel his fingers lock in mine until the screen is dark and the workers come in to clean up between shows. Then Kevin's mouth is moving, but I can't hear anything he is saying.

All I can think about is how I never thought God could love the earth the way I do. But why couldn't it be true that

God may be hurt when we walk by the color purple in a field and don't notice it?

I follow Kevin out to the car and he takes me to Chili's. We eat fajitas and drink Diet Cokes and talk about Celie and Shug and Nettie, about religion and salvation, masculinity and dominance, disruption and changing narratives, and beauty and hope. He tells me about the dorms and keg parties, about classes and professors, about expectations and fear and guilt and longing. I tell him sisterhood must be a dangerous thing, to be so vilified.

I ask questions, and he tells me I have to apply. He tells me I need to live at college, and he tells me how he thinks I can get there.

We stay at Chili's until it closes, and when we leave the building, it's raining. We stand under the awning, looking at how the streetlights reflect the water. He takes my hand, and we run across the empty parking lot to his car, where we talk some more. I ask him to take me to my Grandma's house. I'm scared to be seen, but it's three in the morning, and I feel so safe sequestered in the metal compartment of his vehicle I'm ready to take a risk.

In the symphony of the rain, Kevin looks at me and tells me that when I make it to college, he would like to see me again. "We can go see all the movies made from all the books," he says, "and you can tell me what they get wrong."

I wait until he pulls away to climb the fence and shimmy through the dog door. The house is dark. I cuddle up on the couch with Little One and Sois. I think of Celie and the smile she hides. I think of how everyone just wants to be loved.

I think about how Shug said, "Everything wanna be loved. Us sing and dance, and holla just wanting to be loved. Look at them trees. Notice how the trees do everything people do to get attention . . . Oh, yeah, this field feels like singing!"

I don't want to worship at the cross of a man who kills his son in the name of salvation. I don't want to worship at an altar that denies the poor and the hungry and the enslaved, telling us to wait for heaven to be free. I don't want a God that denies the beauty of women, belying the beauty of the earth. I want the gifts of the mother, and I vow to find my way back to her.

In the morning, I watch Lizbeth eating cereal at Grandma's kitchen table. She asks me why I'm there, and I tell her what I have done.

By noon, everyone at the Field knows I have been out with a college boy, that I have seen a movie, and that the movie was rated R. It's such a connected community it's hard to know who initiated the report. I don't ask Lizbeth, because I don't want to believe my sister betrayed me, but the bottom line is, I have broken too many rules to defend myself and I am clearly beyond redemption. By later that afternoon, I am officially excommunicated.

Mrs. Mitchell looks at me with disgust. "Who do you think you are?" she says.

I have no idea who I am. I watch the girl standing there, talking to Mrs. Mitchell, who is trembling. The girl listening to her is calm and distant. She doesn't say what she is thinking: *If Kevin can live at college, I can live at college.* Knowing this is a possibility makes it possible.

I am banned from all Field activities, and going forth, no one is allowed to speak to me. Since I'm no longer living in my body, this doesn't bother me as much as it would have a few months ago. Like Jezebel, I'd rather be evil than powerless.

I walk down the creaky stairs from Grandpa's old office. I can't find my footing. I want to become a pillar of salt, but I won't look back. I won't say I'm sorry, and I won't say goodbye.

I'd rather be bad than weak.

I ride the bike down the back forty and return it to Tammy. I tell her thank you, but she doesn't speak to me. I have betrayed the rules of the family, and I am no longer welcome in her home.

I walk toward Mother's office, debating whether to go in. I hear a growling sound, like a frightened animal. I look around, but I don't see any animals. I look down at my own body, wondering if the noise came from me. My stomach growls again.

I haven't eaten since Chili's. I recognize this as hunger. I pat my stomach, and it makes a hollow sound, soft, like a drum. *I am hungry.* I pat the words to a rhythm. *I am hungry.*

It will be many hours before my parents drive back up to the Mountain. I stop and listen to what my body is saying: *I am hungry, and I need nourishment.*

I want to go home. I go to the office to find Thomas, whom we used to prank during the early years, when he cared for us on the Mountain. He was Mother's favorite then and has been rising up the ranks of leadership. (One day, he will wear Grandpa's shoes and run the Field differently than Grandpa did. But I don't know this now.) I sense he has the power to bend the protocol of my shunning and the will to do so. I ask him to drive me to the Mountain.

Thomas says he can't do that, but he says he will feed me. I get into his car, and he takes me out to dinner, even though this is not something we're allowed to do. I sit with him at Mimi's Cafe and listen to his tale of salvation, how he doesn't know his own father, but how my grandfather was there for him, how my father was there for him, how they taught him our heavenly Father is there for him, how he is looking forward to becoming a father himself someday, how Grandpa was the man he needed when he was younger, so he will become like Grandpa for those who need him.

"I have never been who anyone wants me to be, but also I'm also not who I want to be," I tell him.

He says to me in a kind voice, though he must know it's not what I want to hear, "You can repent. Remember the prodigal son. And how *God so loved the world, that he gave his only begotten Son, that whosoever believeth in him should—*"

"I'm no one's son," I interrupt, struggling to find words for what no one says. "I'm a daughter, and daughters have to fight by different rules, because God doesn't have a daughter or a wife. He doesn't know what we need."

Thomas looks at me and says it's okay to be confused, but if I can't obey the rules, I should go. "You're driving your cart awfully close to the edge," he tells me. "The chasm is deep, and *the fearful, and unbelieving, and the abominable, and murderers, and whoremongers, and sorcerers, and idolaters,* and all liars, shall have their part in the lake which burneth with fire and brimstone: which is the second death.*"*

"*And whosoever was not found written in the book of life was cast into the lake of fire,*" I reply. "And I'm not written in that book."

Thomas looks sad but tender.

"We are all nomads," I say. "Here until we're not."

"*In my Father's house are many mansions: if it were not so, I would have told you. I go to prepare a place for you,*" he recites.

"I don't believe there is a better place where we will all end up someday. I'm not saying I know where the edge is," I try to explain. "I don't. But I'm willing to fall to find it."

"Go in peace," Thomas says.

As he drives us back to the Field, I take off my shoes. I don't think he notices that I've left them under his front seat as I walk down the back forty for the last time, barefoot, which is against the rules. I climb softly into the back of Dad's truck to wait for my parents to arrive.

Eventually, when they do, I assume they see me sitting here, but they don't speak. Dad starts the engine, and as we drive up the hill, I lie down.

I accept their silence as a gift. It feels like grace.

On the Mountain, no one talks about what has happened or what I will do next. The rhythms of the family go on as before. My excommunication remains, but I don't feel claustrophobic here, the way I did among a throng of people who pretended I didn't exist. While Danny and Becca ride down to the Field with our parents, I stay on the Mountain and wait.

The family drives down the hill early each morning, and they come home late at night, if they come home at all. I stay on the Mountain and watch the sun, noticing the angles and shapes of the shadows it creates.

The days pass in a predictable pattern of light and dark, heat and cold, the days growing longer. A ghost in me is whispering, but I can't yet hear what she is saying. The moments string out, looking substantially the same, but I hold on to the possibility that the next moment might be different.

When I pay close attention, when I really look at what is going on around me, there are, of course, no moments that are the same.

When the Mountain awakens into spring, the bright, generous energy of the sun melts the snow, as if directing the green things of the earth to rise and play their symphony. The sounds of the birds and insects become louder and more distinct. A snow plant peeks its head through the pine needles. I watch it for what feels like days, sitting at my window, open to the caress of the warming breeze, waiting for guidance.

But human time is not mountain time, so I don't know how long it is before I go out to sit next to it, the forgiving soil yielding to my footfall, making dents that look like craters. I am barefoot, so I can feel the earth holding me.

One day, I pick the snow plant. I take it to the kitchen and peel off the red petals, fanning them out into an array of color, like the weddings at the Field in which I was a flower girl. I boil the naked root and then I take the armful of petals outside and fling them onto the pine needles, a gift for the birds, rather than a bride.

I stand in the sun. My shadow looks small and boneless on the holy ground. I don't know how long I can stay here, I don't know how I will leave, and I don't know where I will go when I do. All I know is that I am hungry, and I think I may be able to feed myself with what this mountain is giving me.

I hold the root of the snow plant in my hands and take a bite. I chew slowly and swallow fully. I let my body slide down onto the petal-strewn pine needles, and I eat every last bite of the root.

I think about how migration can be triggered by the angle of sunlight, by a change in temperature or the availability of food. My time to migrate is imminent. I picture the gooseberries next to the willow and decide I will go there first. I locate one of Mother's backpacks and dump out her contents. I will fill it with what I need.

After I cull the gooseberries, I circle around for the rose hips near the log and the chokecherries up above the chapel. When I see a grove of nettles, I brush my fingers in the direction of the spikes to keep them from piercing me, but I will need a barrier to prevent stinging as I snap the stems. I take off my shirt to use it like a glove.

As I'm filling Mother's backpack with nettles, I notice that yerba santa has spread over half the hill. So I fill the rest of the space in the backpack with holy weed and head toward the bunks on the highest plain, where I will make piles from what I have collected.

Being alone becomes who I am. I can't remember it ever being otherwise. I stop brushing my hair. My curls mat into clumps, hanging off my head like ropes. I stop wearing shoes altogether, and my feet become calloused. I don't recognize this version of me, but here she is, birthing into being.

There is no one to tell me what to do or not do. I am more animal than human, scavenging like a primate, not a soldier in the army of God. The family continues to drive down to the Field, and I continue to forage.

I collect a backpack full of acorns that have fallen from the black oak near the mess hall. I use the camp kitchen to boil and blanch them, using the big oven to bake sheet after sheet. I pound them into flour and put it into piles, like little rows of mountains made of dust.

When the labor and the assault of memories make my head spin, I breathe into a paper bag, the way Mother taught me many years ago.

I add water to some of the piles and make them into a paste, patting them into little cakes, frying them up on the grill. I eat them with my fingers while they're still hot, like I never got to do as a child, savoring the way they warm my hands and my lips and my tongue before sliding into my body, nourishing places inside me I had forgotten were there. Then I go back out to collect more, not wanting to let go, now that I have found what I am looking for.

The black oak is covered with lichen, which Mother taught us is really a marriage of algae and fungi, living in symbiosis with each other. Of course, fungi and algae can live independently, but when they join with one another, they give up their previous identities, becoming a community of lichen. I think about our capacity for conformity at the Field, and how we too, have merged into a shared identity.

I look closely at the relationship the lichen have formed with the tree. The lichen isn't a parasite, since it isn't extracting nutrients from this black oak tree. It's just a place to grow. Mother says commensalism isn't the same as parasitism, because no one is harmed in the exchange.

I wonder if she attached herself to the Mountain like the lichen has attached itself to this tree, because it provides the right environment for growth.

It feels like a rotting animal is churning in my belly. I vomit up what I can, cradle the liquid in my hands, and bury it in the earth. With my knees in the dirt, I create my own initiation ceremony, a liturgy born of spontaneity, like the Friends in Aunt Bernice's Quaker circle when they speak what the spirit moves them to say.

I turn on the spigot and fill my hands with water, pouring it over my head like a baptism. I lift my face to feel the wind, testing the air, my hunger, my desire.

Don't look back. Don't ever look back.

But I do.

I turn around and stare down the Mountain, thinking of the biblical Ruth, who migrated to strange lands with Naomi, just to be mothered. I feel Ruth in me. I want to be mothered too.

I am every girl I have ever been: The believer. The invalid. The victim. The fighter. The heretic. Uncivilized. Ravenous. Angry. Wicked. Wild. These girls all sing inside me like a choir.

I look back at my ten-year-old self, staring down the Mountain, lost. I think of her inner compass, incomplete, navigating with the tools she has been given. I know how to use these tools even better now.

That girl was indoctrinated by a cult, but she had a high pain tolerance and a basic knowledge of the region's ecosystem. I think of her sharpening her mind against the silence of the trees. Whatever came up the Mountain, she was watching, breathing, and tasting with her wordless love.

I'll be lost plenty in the coming years. But I will hold on to this.

I take my child self with me down the hill as I walk several miles toward the high desert in search of yucca. When I see the first one, lit in all its glory, I sit next to it, affectionately, like she's a friend. Something of her wildness is alive in me, and I want more.

I eat her flowers raw. Then I carefully peel off a small portion of the fibrous coating, filling Mother's backpack with strands from the stalk, careful not to damage the rest of the plant by what I take with me.

I survey the landscape. *Survive fear. Survive with faith.* I will need shelter. I triangulate to pinpoint a location where I can build.

My compass has always pointed to this Mountain. Where do I belong that isn't here?

I don't have a map, and I can't navigate by the stars during the daylight. I can't go back to the Field or to Grandma's, but I know I won't be able to stay here forever. I need to migrate.

I hike down farther into the desert, where there is no place to hide. I won't be carrying any rocks this time, since

I'm no longer willing to weigh myself down. I sit in the silence of the desert heat, looking straight at the sun, letting it burn into the hollow spaces where my faith used to be. Maybe this silence scared Grandpa. Maybe that's why he stopped coming here.

For he that hath, to him shall be given: and he that hath not, from him shall be taken even that which he hath.

I spend the day eating yucca and prickly pear, watching surprises rise from the desert floor, observing the wildlife as if seeing it for the first time.

Mother tells me to worship the gods of my father, as she tries to worship the gods of her father, but down deep, her liturgy is in these plants, in these insects, in the fabric of this earth, yearning toward mutualism, toward cooperation, toward all she prepared me to receive.

I will have no other gods before me.

Kneeling on the earth, with the smell of our Lord's candle on my hands, I worship the light, reaching for what will sustain me.

What if the earth isn't the devil's domain? What if nothing is wrong with the world as we know it, if nothing is wasted in nature or in love?

But loving a place isn't enough. I walk back up to the Mountain, carrying the word as I have heard it.

Soon, I will go, and I won't be invited back. Not even to Lizbeth's wedding.

It will be many years until I find my way back to this mountain, until I will check back in on the Mountain, as an old friend. And I will do this over and over, because Mother Earth doesn't turn women who look back into pillars of salt.

When I leave, I won't say goodbye. I'll simply slither out my bedroom window, with the stories of Rahab, Tamar, Ruth, and Bathsheba tucked like a knife in my sheath, making my exit like a scar.

And I'll leave the window open.

Lichens

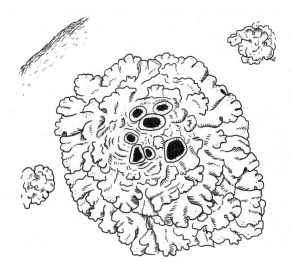

Lichens are a complex life-form, a symbiotic partnership of two separate organisms, a fungus and an alga. The outer skin and internal structure of a lichen is made of fungal hyphae, while the strands inside the lichen contain individual cells of algae.

Lichens provide shelter and food for other organisms, by way of materials they can use to build their nests. They are found in a vast diversity of habitats and climates, from the desert to the forest, and get all the nutrients they need from rain and the surrounding air. When lichens grow on rocks, the chemicals that they release contribute to the slow process of rock breakdown and soil formation. Lichens can be used for food, clothing, dyes, perfumes, medicines, poisons, *tanning agents, bandaging, and absorbent materials. You can also feed them to dogs.*

Lichens are usually the first type of organism to appear after a fire. They can survive when plants can't and can grow on rough surfaces, like rocks.

I DROVE UP TO THE MOUNTAIN recently to forage for elderberries, because they were the most healing plant in season, and Mother needs healing. I dialed my childhood phone number, and George answered. He was kind to me and said that, yes, I was welcome to visit. George and his piano still live in our old home, and soon, one of the boys I lived with the summer of the Night Stalker will be moving in to run the retreat center, which is now available for rental to outside groups.

I was early, and the gate was locked when I got there, so I left a text message and climbed over the gate. I hiked to the upper camp in the late spring snow, where I made a fire and slept alone in the upper camp bunkhouse. On my way out the next day, George gave me a stack of Mother's coloring books, along with sheets of her notes.

Despite decades of living in the outside world, it felt as if I had arrived back home, returning to grace, like the prodigal son.

I stopped in at the historic Wrightwood Museum, where a docent in her early seventies introduced herself as Barbara and encouraged me to look around and to ask her if I had any questions. I always have questions, but I held my tongue and riffled through the pictures, looking for images that could teach me something about what this place was before we got here. There were photographs of the lodge that used to be here in the 1920s, with a pool and an ice-skating rink, all let go during the Great Depression. I thought about what this community looked like when my grandfather was a very young man and would bring boys up to sleep on the Mountain.

I apparently showed enough interest that Barbara asked me if I grew up here.

"Not in Wrightwood itself," I said, "but a few miles up the hill, at a camp, before it was much of a camp."

"Near the station?"

"Near there, yes."

"Did you know the Dowds?" she asked. "They used to live up that way. Mrs. Dowd was quite the naturalist. Legendary. You'd remember her if you met her. Smart as a whip, that one."

I considered lying, telling her that was before my time, but I've mostly stopped running from what formed me. "Yeah, that's my mom."

"Well, Lord have mercy, what a day. Mrs. Dowd is your God-given mother?"

I nodded.

"You don't look a thing like her, honey. Never would've guessed. She was a spitfire, that one. More energy than I've ever seen in a woman, and, Lord, what a whirlwind of knowledge she had in her. Knew the names and uses for all of God's creations, and never needed notes to tell it. I was born here, and shoulda known better, but it was your mama taught me everything I know about this mountain, God bless her."

I've never heard my mother mention Barbara, or any women friends.

"How is your mama these days, love?" Barbara asked.

"She's good," I said politely.

Never put your hands or feet anywhere you can't see. If you need to step over a log, step up on it, look, then step down. If you encounter a black bear, don't look him in the eye. Just back away slowly. If you encounter a brown bear, roll up in a ball. Either way, don't be afraid. Be competent.

"What a trip," Barbara exclaimed. "To think you were up the hill the whole time. What a trip! Worked with your mama for years. Never thought she had children. My word, I just never would have guessed."

My mother is still full of contradictions. She respected the natural world and could identify everything in this region, but she didn't recognize her children as animals or protect us from the predators she could have known were there, had she paid attention.

For years, I wanted to get as far away from the Mountain as I could, and I was certain I would never come back.

When I was sixteen, one of the women whose houses I cleaned gave me a brochure and an application to a competitive college, where she said I would thrive. I filled it out in pencil, including a poem as my statement of purpose, and after my excommunication, mailed it from the post office in Wrightwood. An admissions officer there sent my application over to a small liberal arts school in Claremont, which she knew embraced unconventional students. The college offered me full financial funding, so when I was seventeen, I moved into the dorms there.

After I left the Mountain, my family moved down to the valley to live next to the Field. That way, Mother could more effectively run their school and my younger siblings could be more fully incorporated into the community of the Field, so that they wouldn't stray like I did.

But in the next three years, Becca and Danny left anyway. My parents still haven't forgiven me.

While I excelled academically, reading so widely and voraciously that my professors introduced me to their families and treated me like a friend, I had no idea how to engage socially with my peers in the outside world. So while I was still in college, I married an older Quitter and rapidly gave birth to four babies.

In my twenties, I moved fast and furiously through every marker of adulthood, inured to the kind of pandemonium that makes most people dizzy. All I wanted was to keep moving, to keep migrating, to be an animal and trust my instincts for survival. I didn't want to belong to anything or count on anyone.

It's easy to mistake chaos for aliveness.

Burying the memories of my childhood was how I stayed in motion, how I survived fear and battled faith.

And then, when I thought I had outrun my upbringing, my mother's terminal illness brought me to my knees.

What we bury grows.

During the hearings of the Field's only public sexual abuse scandal in 2006, my parents moved to a large gated senior community in the desert. My mother, who had become the principal of the Field's in-house school when her father died, was technically in charge when one of the male leaders violated several preteen boys, who eventually banded together and reported it. She was subpoenaed and asked questions she never thought she would have to answer.

The leader pleaded guilty, and Mother wasn't found accountable, but my parents stayed in the desert anyway—away from the Field, away from the Mountain, away from their people and the work to which they had dedicated their whole lives.

And now Mother is dying. She has been dying for a long time, but it feels to me that she is nowhere near dead.

I visit her regularly now, and part of me feels as if I'm still begging for attention—or love. Maybe they're the same thing.

I think of all the things I can't say to Mother. I can't even take off my sweater, or she'll see my tattoos, further evidence that I have defiled God's temple.

She has had difficulty forgiving me for things great and small that I've done to disappoint her. I am not the daughter she wanted, and she says I'm not the kind of woman she raised me to be. But I keep coming back, because I *am* my mother's daughter. And even if she can't see it, I am clearly the woman she raised me to be.

The cultural conversation around ecology has changed since I was raised on the Mountain, and much of what Mother once taught me has become common sense. More people now recognize that nature is an interconnected whole, and that organisms can't be understood in isolation.

A fit organism won't stop at survival. It attaches to what it needs to grow and thrive. Like the lichen, we can make a life in places where we couldn't survive alone.

When I drive up to the wilderness preserve I frequently visit, I see a little church with a big banner out front, which, in bright-blue letters, forms the words FREE FOOD AND COMMUNITY AFTER EVERY SUNDAY SERVICE. I picture congregants sitting together at long tables, sharing sustenance and conversation, forming connections.

It pleases me that there are churches that recognize how hungry we all are.

But I've never stopped by. It is still hard for me to trust a group, even one that offers to feed me. When I am hungry, I eat from whatever is growing around me, because that's what I know. When I feel lonely or disconnected, I look to the intelligence of nature for connection. Attachment is a survival skill. As is wildness.

As I drive down the one-way dirt road toward a home I share with multiple species, I envision what I will do when I arrive: I will walk barefoot through a mile of forest, and then I will sit still and listen to the sounds of the mountain, teeming with life. I visualize being cleansed, like Grandma felt cleansed, walking near the roses in the garden of her Lord.

I have come back to Mother Nature, because she has shown me a wider definition of community. Connecting to her connects me to myself. As I eat from the earth, I consecrate what I devour, because there is still some wild left in me, and even darkness can be a gift.

We are made for recovery.

I frequently hike off trail, without a phone or a GPS device, and sometimes, when I don't know where I am, I think I might be lost. But I don't panic. I stop, look around, root into my surroundings, and breathe.

ACKNOWLEDGMENTS

I AM GRATEFUL FOR WHERE I come from, for the gifts of community (human and non-human), for those who have stood by me on this circuitous journey, and the many (named and unnamed) who held me while I lived or re-lived these stories. More specifically, I am grateful to:

The Breeze students and my colleagues at Chaffey College for inspiring my work in journalism.

Dan Jones for choosing *Love in the Time of Low Expectations* for the 2020 Modern Love column that started this ball rolling.

Lucinda Halpern, for guiding me through the process that brought this book to life.

My tough-love editor Betsy Gleick and the entire Algonquin team, including Brunson Hoole, Mae Zhang McCauley, Michael McKenzie, Marisol Salaman, and Debra Linn.

Elizabeth Johnson for her thorough copyediting and being such a joy to work with.

Angela Cardinale and Vicki Tulacro for books, food, friendship, and laughter and for a lifetime of sisterhood. (I wouldn't be here without you!)

Deckard Hodge for reading early drafts, our unforgettable graffiti expedition, and the buttress of a decades-long friendship.

Aram Mitchell, for being my accountability partner

through the process of writing *Forager* (and for the evolution to forever friend and family).

Noel Besuzzi, my cousin and photographer extraordinaire, for the official author photo, numerous creative collaborations, and enduring support.

Abbie Moore for cheerleading, blankets, snacks, and undying devotion.

Emily St. Martin for her magnificent motivation, for discussing dozens of memoirs with me, for encouraging me to have higher expectations for myself, and for being present as a friend and fellow writer. (Love you forever and always!)

Joanna Lord for her indefatigable energy and friendship, for cultivating a creative community, and for building my website.

Barny Peake for kintsugi.

Meredith Talusan and the Fairest Writers' Book Club for numerous conversations on craft and providing a community of writers who support one another.

Stephanie Couch and Leigh Estabrooks for demonstrating how to thrive in the work of invention education and for mentoring me into a woman who asks for what she wants.

Jen Pastiloff for her constant courage and tireless devotion to supporting a community of artists.

Patrick Jimenez for teaching me to think outside the box and for sharing the love language of dogs.

Rob Sullivan for years and years of lithography and putting up with my chaos.

Ted Younglove for asking what I need and frequently delivering it—without expectations.

Drew Philp, for expansive and ongoing literary and life conversations.

Rebecca Trawick and Roman Stollenwerk for the Wignall Museum and the Reunion Exhibition.

Leslie Adams and Elizabeth Keller for breaking open the stories of the skies and buoying me when I was unmoored—and for all the women of the Moon Circle for celebrating sisterhood.

My yogi sisters Monica, Nicole, Mari, Tracy, Sarah, Sharon, Amy, Olivia, and Jenna—for years of practicing together and encouraging me to breathe.

Gratitude as plentiful as the stars in the sky and the sands on the shore for my family—Lori, Wendy, and Mikey for sharing their memories and putting up with the discrepancies of mine; Linda for mothering me into her family when I was eighteen; Scott for having my back from the beginning; Summer, River, Storm, and Zephyr for being a constant source of wonderment and pride; and Holden for guiding us into the future.

And a particular recognition, respect, and love for my late mother, Arlis, and my late grandmothers Ruth and Ivy for demonstrating a lifetime of scrappiness and for teaching me there is sustenance everywhere—you just have to know what you're looking for.